The Chausathi Yoginis of Hirapur: from Tantra to Tourism

The Chausathi Yoginis of Hirapur: from Tantra to Tourism

Dr. Adyasha Das

BLACK EAGLE BOOKS
2019

Immediately after this, the book took shape. Based on my research and information I collected from museums in several places, I have tried to demystify the relatively unknown Chausathi Yoginis of Hirapur. Several rare aspects of this temple intrigued me. The Yogini Cult, Tantrik in nature and tantra itself, projecting the efficacy of magical rituals and spell, sounds and gestures, is intertwined deeply with rural and tribal traditions. There is a diverse range of attitudes toward the tantric traditions, ranging from viewing it as a path to liberation to the relatively widespread associations of the tantric traditions with sorcery and libertine sexuality. In Hinduism, the tantra tradition is most often associated with its goddess tradition called Shaktism, followed by Shaivism and Vaishnavism. In this temple, every male deity except Shiva are replaced by a female counterpart including Ganesha all of them representing varied qualities. The Yoginis were believed to impart magical powers to their worshippers:

These powers included:

anima (the ability to become very small),

laghima (the power to levitate and to be able to leave your body at will),

garima (the power to become very heavy),

mahima (the power to become large in size),

istiva (the power to control the body and mind of oneself and others),

parakamya (the power to make others do your biding),

vasitva (the power to control the five elements) and

kamavasayitva (the power to be able to fulfill all your desires) (Dehejia).

According to the Archeological Survey of India the temple came to be known in 1953(Mahapatra 1953).

This seems strange considering the close proximity of the temple to the state capital Bhubaneswar. I have visited the temple uncountable times, mostly alone but often with friends and have enjoyed the quiet isolation that has been thrust upon not just this temple but the cult as well. The most beautiful Yogini temple among all, sixty three Yoginis are enshrined here. One statue is missing.

In my pursuit of the Yoginis, I visited the Chaunsathi Yogini temple at Khajuraho. The Yogini temple is unique, an open-air quadrangular structure. The shrines are small, ordinary cells, roofed by a sikhara of an elementary form. I found this the most primitive of all Yogini temples in construction and unique in being quadrangular and not circular like the others.

The Chausath Yogini temple at Khajuraho

The breath-taking beauty of the Chausath Yogini temple at Mitaoli is a rare experience I never wished to miss. I was at the Indian Institute of Tourism and Travel Management, Gwalior to participate in the Euro-Asia conference. I decided to visit the Chausath Yogini Temple, Morena, also known as Ekattarso Mahadeva Temple. This is an 11th-century temple located in Morena district in the state of Madhya Pradesh. It is one of the few such Yogini temples in the country which is in a good condition. The temple is formed by a circular wall with 64 chambers and an open mandapa in the centre, separated by a courtyard which is circular in shape, where Shiva is deified.

I started out early for Morena, driving through the Chambal valley. A non-descript village and an insignificant hill disappointed me on my arrival. While climbing up the hill, I almost stumbled upon a huge python slithering past. The driver told me that the hills were infested with poisonous snakes. But I was amazed at the sheer beauty of the temple at the top and stopped for few minutes to let in the feeling of wonder at having seen yet another abode of the Yoginis.

This book is a compilation of my research and readings on the Chausathi Yogini temple at Hirapur. This book was motivated by the desire to delve deeply into the tantric roots in which the Yogini cult is embedded and to link it to the significance of this site as a potential cultural tourism destination.

The Chausath Yogini temple, Mitaoli

Chausathi Yoginis: An Introduction

The Yogini shrines of India are steeped in historical grandeur, mythology and cultural significance. Viewed independently, each of these monuments appears to be a conundrum. Their common circular plan constitutes a legitimate variant when compared to other legitimate Hindu architecture. A close study of the temples however, reveals considerable diversity among them. The list of the sixty-four yoginis at the different temples do not correspond to each other, neither to any recognized Puranic list of Yoginis. The cult of sixty-four yoginis was at a time widely prevalent in the central and eastern parts of India along with other cults of Sakta-tantricism.

The culture of sixty-four Yoginis was the exuberant expression of an extreme form of tantricism in about 8th century AD when the occult and esoteric Sadhana reached the highest peak. The origin of the pantheon of sixty-four yoginis is shrouded in mystery. The vedic and post-vedic literature mention the names of some individual yoginis, but never sixty-four manifestations together. Through the process of transformation the cult came into existence and exerted an important niche in the Sakta-tantric pantheon. The puranas and Upa-puranas which are the source of different cults are referred to find out the origin of sixty-four yoginis, who are basically the mother-goddesses. (Origin of Tantricism and Sixty-Four Yogini Cult in Orissa - Dr. Janmejay Choudhury)

The Shakti cult came into prominence during the period of Shankaracharya around 9th Century AD. There are four major shrines of the Sixty-four Yogini (Chausathi Yogini, among other spellings) in India (named for 64 legendary yoginis), two in Odisha and two in Madhya Pradesh. One of the most impressive yogini temples in Odisha is the ninth century CE hypaethral Chausathi Yogini Temple located at Hirapur in Khurda district, 15 km south of Bhubaneshwar. Another hypaethral sixty-four yogini temple in Odisha is the Chausathi Yogini Pitha in Ranipur-Jharial, near Titilagarh in Balangir district. Two images of the Sixty-four Yoginis are missing from this temple.

Two notable yogini temples in Madhya Pradesh are the ninth-century Chaunsath Yogini Temple to the southwest of the western group of temples in Khajuraho, near Chhatarpur in Chhatarpur District, and the 10th century CE Chaunsath Yogini Mandir in Bhedaghat, near Jabalpur in Jabalpur district. The iconographies of the yogini images in the different yogini temples are not uniform. In the Hirapur temple, all yogini images are with their vahanas (vehicles) and in standing posture, with intricate coiffures and distinct sets of jewellery. In Ranipur-Jharial temple the yogini images are in dancing posture. In Bhedaghat temple, yogini images are seated in Lalitasana.

The majority of scholars and researchers agree that Tantrism flourished at some point of time between 5th and 6th century. There are ample references to Tantrism in the ancient Vedic literature. In course of time, evidence of the application of tantra in Hinduism, Buddhism and Jainism has also been established. The latter, Buddhism is popularly known as Tantric Buddhism. It flourished between 8th and 12th century AD

Odisha is known the world over for the Jagannath cult which has gained wide popularity. However this land has been a pot-pourri for multiple sects since aeons. Much before the spread of Jagannath cult in Odisha, the area was known to be a throbbing hub of Shaivaite activities and prior to that a stimulating cauldron of tantric and shakti practices. Distinct marks of Buddhism are also visible in Odisha before it got swayed by tantric practices.

The evolution of the Tantric culture started noticeably in two places in Odisha, one at Hirapur and the other at Ranipur Jharial in Balangir. At the time of the advent of Buddhism, Tantricism was highly developed in Odisha. Buddhist Pantheons developed and prospered highly in Odisha. Gradually the Buddhist tantra gave way to the Hindu tantra. Tara of the Buddhist pantheon became identified as Mangala Nila Saraswati and later as Ramachandi.

Though much of Buddhist and Shakti cults consequently lost identity having merged themselves in the evolving religious cults of that time, they have left their imprints on the sands of time in forms of architecture and vague references in religious scriptures. The Yogini cult is one such cult which having found its origin from the Shakti form of worship, prospered well in the 8th century Odisha. The famous 64 yogini temple of Hirapur is a memento of the significance of this now extinct cult from Odisha.

Not much is known about the yogini cult and the various tantric practices undertaken by them is still shrouded in mysticism. In fact so much secrecy was maintained about the practices of this cult, that mere mention of this term would create awe and fear among people. The main reason behind this, probably, is the secrecy of the Yogini cult which is kept in dark from the common mass. Also the images of the yoginis are sculpted with demonic expressions and other dark attributes which evoked fear among the devotees. When the yoginis are depicted in sculpture or described in text, they often have the heads of various birds such as: parrots, hawks, peacocks, eagles, pigeons, and owls.

Apart from this, yoginis are associated with cemeteries and battle- -fields where they are said to devour the dead. They were worshipped by kings and soldiers before going on a battle for good luck and victory. Yoginis find mention in the Rudra Upanishad where it is stated that Lord Shiva after slaying Jalandhara summoned the Yoginis (Sapta- matrika) to the battlefield and asked them to devour the flesh of the demon and drink the blood.

Origin of The Yogini Cult

The Yogini tradition is essentially tantric in nature and therefore has strong connections to rural and tribal traditions. However references about these deities have been found in puranic literature too. That the cult of sixty-four yoginis was widely prevalent is evident from several lists of sixty-four yoginis recorded in different texts. The Kalika purana, Skanda purana, Brihadnandikeswara Purana, Cansatha yogini namavali, Chandi purana of Sarala Das, Durgapuja, Brihndla Tantra, Bata Avakasa of Balaram Das and other texts contain the list of sixty-four yoginis. They are:

1. Chhaya,
2. Maya,
3. Narayani,
4. Brahmayani,
5. Bhairavi,
6. Maheswari,
7. Rudrayani,
8. Baseli,
9. Tripura,
10. Ugratara,
11. Charchika,
12. Tarini,
13. Ambika Kumari,
14. Bhagabati,
15. Nila,
16. Kamala,
17. Santi,
18. Kanti,
19. Ghatabari,
20. Chamunda,
21. Chandrakanti,
22. Madhavi,
23. Kachikeswari,
24. Anala,
25. Rupa,
26. Barahi,
27. Nagari,
28. Khechari,
29. Bhuchari,
30. Betali,
31. Kalinjari,
32. Sankha,

33. Rudrakali,
34. Kalavati,
35. Kankali,
36. Bukuchai,
37. Bali,
38. Dohini,
39. Dwarini,
40. Sohini,
41. Sankata Tarini,
42. Kotalai,
43. Anuchhaya,
44. Kechamukhi Samuha,
45. Ullaka,
46. Samasila,
47. Mudha,
48. Dakhinai,
49. Gopali,
50. Mohini,
51. Kamasena,
52. Kapali,
53. Uttarayani,
54. Trailokya Byapini,
55. Trilochana,
56. Nimai,
57. Dakeswari,
58. Kamala,
59. Ramayani,
60. Anadi Shakti,
61. Balakshatrayani,
62. Brahmani,
63. Dharani,
64. Matangi.

Mythology apart, the origin of the Yoginis appears to have been in small, rural villages. They are local village goddesses, grama devatis, who look over the welfare of an individual village. Through Tantricism, these local deities were able to gain new forms and vitality as a group of goddesses who could impart magical powers to their worshippers.

In the villages of Odisha, the Yoginis are the favoured deities. Each grama devi, be she Ramchandi, Shyamkali, Harachandi, Tarini, Viraja, Bhagavati, Durgamata, Sarala, Bhadrakali, Kamakhya, Bhabani, Mangala etc., presides over the welfare of the village. These village goddesses seem to have been gradually transformed and consolidated into potent numerical groupings of sixty-four (sometimes eighty-one, sometimes forty-two) acquiring thereby a totally different character. It was Tantricism that elevated these local deities and gave them new form and vigour as a group of goddesses who could bestow magical powers with a view to destruction of the enemies.

There are four main traditions that are associated with the cult of the yoginis and how they developed from their tribal beginnings and became integrated into orthodox beliefs. All four of the traditions revolve around the idea that the yoginis were minor divinities to greater goddesses. The first tradition is the idea of the yoginis as aspects of the Devi or Great Goddess. The yoginis were said to be formed from different parts of the Devi, including her voice, sweat, navel, forehead, cheeks, lips, ears, limbs, toe nails, womb, and her anger. The second tradition is the idea that the yoginis are attendant deities of the Great Goddess. This tradition is thought to have developed from the earlier tradition of Shiva and his gana attendants. The third tradition focuses on the yoginis as acolytes of the Great Goddess: the matrukas. This tradition describes the yoginis as being born of eight mothers and formed into eight groups. The fourth and final tradition centers on the thought of the yoginis as patrons of the goddess of the Kaulas.

Yogini Worship

The worship of Chausathi Yoginis in Odisha started around 800 AD and flourished till 1300 AD. The cult is influenced by Tantrik rituals and a great deal of the worship was conducted to achieve powers of black magic. The number 64, being a multiple of 8, was considered to have magical powers in the numerology of India. Devotees who performed this worship were known to conduct the Shava Chhedan ceremony — meaning the beheading of a dead body as the ultimate symbol of detachment from earthly desires. The members of this cult never harmed living beings and never conducted animal or human sacrifices.

Until 1500 AD, there are references in history to the widespread following of this cult. Yogini worshippers would ask for corpses from poor families with a promise of a grand funeral and provide this after their Shava or corpse ritual was over.

In Yogini worship, the Tantrik symbol is a chakra with 64 spokes in the wheel. Each spoke represents one Yogini, a form of Shakti. In most of the well-conserved temples, the sculptures of Yoginis are intact and none of them are erotic as in other temples. This is because this cult did not believe in sex as a path to self discovery.

But in later centuries, owing to the scary nature of the rituals and because of the growing stronghold of the Bhakti movement all over India — which preached love of God as the finest path to self realisation — this cult died a slow death, and remained only confined to small pockets of India. Thus, today, several Yogini temples are lying in a state of utter neglect, dilapidated and neglected. However the element of fear still persists and even tourists are sometimes believe these scary interpretations and are hesitant to enter the precincts of the Yogini temples.

However, Yogini temples in Hirapur and Ranipur Jharial are in excellent conditions even today.

The earliest evidence of Yogis and their spiritual tradition, states Karel Werner, is found in the Kesin hymn of the Vedas, where these Yogins are praised. However, there is no mention that these Vedic era Yogi's included women. Scholars note that some ancient Vedic sages (Rishis) were women. A female rishi is known as a rishika.

The term Yogini has been in used in medieval times to refer to a woman who belongs to the Gorakshanath-founded Nath Yogi tradition. They usually belong to the Shaiva tradition, but some Nathas belong to the Vaishnava tradition. In both cases, states David Lorenzen, they practice Yoga and their principal God tends to be Nirguna, that is a God that is without form and semi-monistic, influenced in the medieval era by the Advaita Vedanta school of Hinduism, Madhyamaka school of Buddhism, as well as Tantra and Yogic practices. Female yoginis were a large part of this tradition, and many 2nd-millennium paintings depict them and their Yoga practices. David Lorenzen states that the Nath yogis have been very popular with the rural population in South Asia, with medieval era tales and stories about Nath yogis continuing to be remembered in contemporary times, in the Deccan, western and northern states of India and in Nepal

In medieval mythology such as Kathasaritsagara, Yogini is also the name of a class of females with magical powers, fairies who are sorceresses sometimes enumerated as 8, 60, 64 or 65.

In real life, historical evidence on Yogini Kaulas suggests that Yogini tradition in Hinduism, who practiced Yoga philosophy and Tantra, was well established by the 10th century. This development was not limited to Hinduism, and included Yoginis in Buddhist tantra traditions. Though the leaders of the modern Yoga-asana & meditation tradition have often been male, the vast majority of modern practitioners are female.

Chausathi Yogini temple, Hirapur

In Search of the Yoginis: The Yogini Trail

A woman dedicated to the pursuit of spiritual knowledge and mystical insight, or a Yogini, has many faces: from devotional to demure and from fiery to fierce, all of these can be embraced under the rubric of a Yogini. Yogini is a term that finds reference in several texts related to Hinduism and Buddhism where its literal meaning is "shaman" or wisdom seer (rishi), a definition that could just as easily be interpreted as "alchemist". Some of the greatest of the ancient rishis were in fact women.

In a wider and general context, a Yogini is a human, a woman who, through the practice of Yoga, may possess supernatural powers, including the ability to transcend the normal aging process via internalization of the reproductive power known as urdhva-retas (upward refinement of the seed-force) and even death, attaining divya sharira (immortal divine body).

Though the leaders of the modern Yoga-asana & meditation tradition have often been male, the vast majority of modern practitioners are female, including many who have attained mastery via steadfast awareness through the Shakti sensations of menses, fertility, childbirth, and breastfeeding. In the Shakta branch of hinduism, creation myths place the Divine Feminine at their center, taking the Tantric view that the nature of the Cosmos (or Macrocosm) is reflected in the human body (or Microcosm), and it is the Female who gestates and gives birth to new life. "Only the female can awaken the muladhara chakra (the seat of the Kundalini-shakti) via fertility and sexuality; the male must use Kriya Yoga".

In some branches of Tantra Yoga, ten wisdom goddesses (or dakinis) serve as models for a Yogini's disposition and behavior. In the mythological context, the word Yogini may indicate an advanced Yoga practitioner who is one or more of the following:

A female who is an associate or attendant of Durga, a fierce aspect of the Divine Feminine, who slays illusion and delusion through insight and liberation.

In several Tantric cults, the term refers to an initiated female who may take part in maithuna tantric rituals. According to the Hatha-Yoga-Pradipika text, a yogini is more specifically a woman initiate, who can preserve her own genital ejaculate (rajas) and contain the male semen (bindu) by means of the practice of the vajroli-mudra, also practiced in reverse by advanced yogis.

Yogini Temples

The Yogini cult has its origin in the simple tribal and folk tradition of India that, by the 7th-8th centuries AD, in conjunction with the "Sakta-Tantric" form, meaning the worship of the Mother Goddess combined with certain magical rituals, had acquired a more definite shape. A large body of Tantric texts and a similar number of shrines found in various parts of the country clearly reveal that several inexhaustible attempts made by its exponents and followers went a long way to popularize this esoteric cult between the 9th and 12th century.

Some later inscriptions found in certain Yogini temples further indicate that the cult was practiced even in the 16th century. It is still not clear as to when exactly the Yogini cult bowed out of limelight, and equally intriguing as to why its temples were abandoned. The entire phenomenon of Yogini worship and the construction of temples has its roots outside the folds of orthodox Brahminical tradition. The Yogini in the shape of a Sakta-Tantric cult came into existence in the 7th-8th century AD. It continued to flourish as an important manifestation of Sakta Tantricism. This cult with primitive ideas on the efficacy of magical rituals and spells, sounds and gestures, is a movement that has a deep connection with rural and tribal traditions. If we were to look for the origin of the Yoginis, we must turn to the simple village cults and to the gram devis, the local village goddesses.

The remains of Yogini temples in various parts of the country clearly reveal that the exponents and followers of this esoteric cult made vigorous attempts to popularize it and this cult was of impelling and vital significance from the 9th to the 12th century. Nine Yogini temples discovered so far are distributed in Odisha, Madhya Pradesh, Uttar Pradesh and in Tamil Nadu. Unfortunately, with the ravage of time, only few of the Yogini temples survive today and Odisha has the distinction of preserving two of these outstanding temples – one at Hirapur, a picturesque village near Bhubaneswar and another at Ranipur-Jharial in Bolangir district.

The Legends

In the ancient scriptures, Yoginis are often depicted as consorts of 'Yogis', and like their male companions practiced 'Yoga' (meditation) to gain mastery over science and acquire magical powers. "Kaula Marga", a tantric form of worship further includes Yoginis of different categories in its "Cakra" (circle) associated with lord Shiva.

The Cakra is alternatively known as "Yogini Cakra", "Kaula Cakra" (the circle of time) or the "Bhairavi Cakra" (the circle of Bhairavi, the female companion of the terrifying form of Shiva known as "Bhairava"). The 'Marga', or path, that defines five ways to perform penance to attain liberation and happiness are 'Matsya' (fish), 'Mamsa' (meat), 'Mudra' (parched grain), 'Madya' (liquor) and 'Maithuna' (sexual intercourse). A large collection of historical texts mention that to attain 'Siddhi' (spiritual powers), the 'Sadhakas' (the Tantric worshippers) unanimously offered flesh, blood and wine to the Yoginis, a tradition still in practice in several parts of Odisha. Devotees offer all these things to most of the village goddesses on important festive occasions, in times of crises, and each time these goddesses manifest themselves in dreams or otherwise to the devotees, demanding such sacrifices.

Often, the Sadhakas took recourse to Maithuna to attain the power of the Yoginis. According to the Kaula path, women of lower caste such as the 'Rajaki' (washerwomen), 'Carmakari' (leather worker), 'Vesya' (prostitute), 'Matangi' (an outcaste) and 'Madhumati' (vintner's caste) are the most suitable partners in the ritual of Maithuna. It further suggests that Maithuna practiced along with yoga leads to the most consummate and soul-lifting physical experience.

Hirapur, near Bhubaneswar, Odisha

The Yogini Temple, also known as the "Mahamaya Temple", has an ambience that is quite vibrant. The temple conveys an impression of the overwhelming power of its sixty-four Yoginis. Mahamaya, the presiding deity of the temple is found adorned with red cloth and vermilion. The deity continues to be worshipped by the local villagers.

The Hirapur Temple, quaint and delicate, is the smallest of the Yogini temples in India. It measures only thirty feet in diameter, and is hardly eight feet high. The temple is built of coarse sandstone blocks with laterite as its foundation. The Yoginis are carved out of fine-grained gray chlorite. The inner walls of the temples have sixty-four niches with sixty Yoginis still in place.

The small central pavilion has eight niches. Three of these have the images of the remaining of the sixty-four Yoginis,(one statue is missing) while the other four have images of the Bhairavas depicted with erect phalluses as is customary of the images of Shiva in Odisha. The images are about two feet tall, and the niches, in which they are placed, were probably treated as miniature shrines.

The construction of the Yogini temple of Hirapur was initiated by the Bhauma and Somavamsi rulers of Odisha who were known for their tolerance, liberal philosophy and eclecticism. Their rule, which lasted from mid-8th to mid-10th century AD, has been depicted as the 'Golden Age' mainly due to their contributions in the fields of philosophy and literature. During this period, there was a gradual amalgamation of Shaivism (worship of Shiva), Shaktism (worship of the Mother Goddess) and the Vajrayana, or Tantric form of Mahayana Buddhism in the region. It is believed that the Yogini Temple at Hirapur was built towards the end of the Bhauma rule, in the 9th century AD

The sculptures of Hirapur temple are extraordinarily beautiful. Faces are delicately carved often with a gentle smile and with coiffures of various styles and heavily ornamented. The architecture of this temple combines a highly original sculptural tradition with extraordinary craftsmanship.

A visit to the Yogini temple at Hirapur marks only the beginning of the journey into Odisha's mysterious past. It also throws light on the role the worship of feminine cults played in promoting harmony through the synthesis of major religious traditions of medieval Odisha.

The Cradle of the Yogini Cult

Simple circular enclosures without a roof are an unusual phenomenon among the religious shrines in India. In addition, the circular walls of these enclosures have niches that enshrine sixty-four female images known as "Yoginis". These shrines are referred to as the "Chausathi" (sixty-four) Yogini temples, and the cult associated with them is known as the Yogini cult.

In some religious texts, Yoginis are also referred to as the attendant deities of the Great Goddess. In contrast, another tradition categorized the 64 Yoginis into potent numeral groupings of 8 forms - those that signify the eight Great Goddesses or the "Asta Matrikas" The images of these Asta Matrikas are widely found in India, especially in Odisha in their larger-than-life forms.

While some of the Yoginis of Hirapur are portrayed as huntresses with bows and arrows, others are shown balancing on a pair of wheels, or playing a drum. Most of them have two hands, but a few are also shown with four. Some of them are poised over a mount that could commonly be a fish, parrot, turtle, frog, snake, scorpion, rat, or a decapitated male head, an archer, to name a few. Some of the Yoginis also have non-human faces of animals such as the horse, ass, rabbit, elephant and lion.

Witchcraft

A number of ancient texts recount terrifying stories highlighting the sorcery or witchcrafts aspect of the Yoginis. According to these stories, Yoginis could acquire certain magical powers with which they could transform human beings into animals and birds. A few other stories talk of a category of witches referred to as 'Dakinis', known for their ability to fly, besides their appetite for human flesh.

In Odisha, the ancient practice of witchcraft is still practiced. Among the Santals of Mayurbhanj district, the Santali witches often leave behind their husbands in bed in the midst of the night to assemble in a forest. Completely naked, they spend the rest of the night dancing and singing with 'bongas' (spirits or deities) and lions as their partners. At the break of dawn, they return to their beds, back to being what they originally were. The Santals believe that the 'talent' for witchcraft is not innate, but is attained through strict discipline.

Legend of Chandi Purana

The 'Chandi Purana', a 15th century AD text, written by Sarala Das of Odisha, refers to Yoginis as forms of the 'Devi' or the Supreme Goddess of the 'Saktas', based on the story of the Goddess 'Chandi' or 'Durga' killing 'Mahisasura' or the buffalo-demon and is a clear reflection of the extreme form of Tantrism practiced in coastal Odisha of those times. According to the text, the Goddess Chandi is said to have liberated numerous number of female soldiers known as Yoginis, who were excessively fond of flesh, blood, bone and marrow. To fulfill these desires, the soldiers fought incessantly with the demons till they were killed and could be consumed. The text states that numerous goats, rams and buffaloes were killed every day to propitiate the Goddess Sarala and the Yoginis.

Vajrayana Buddhism

The Vajrayana or the Tantric form of Buddhism, which evolved against the principles of earlier Buddhism preached by the Buddha himself, had laid great emphasis on the theory of emancipation. The preachers of Vajrayana Buddhism redefined 'Nirvana' (liberation) as 'Shunya' (void), 'Vijnana' and 'Mahasukha' (extreme pleasure) that could be achieved by embracing a woman. In this newly restructured nirvana, women were designated as 'Shakti', and their union with the 'Sadhaka' came to be known as yoga.

Further, Vajrayana Buddhists were empowered to violate laws, kill human beings, and seduce women. They propounded a common slogan - identical actions by which mortals struggling for hundreds of billions of cycles could liberate the 'Yogin' (the Enlightened Man).

Khajuraho is one of the ten most predominant seats of Tantra practice. According to the Tantra tradition, there are certain special sites that are charged with spiritual energy, enabling the seeker to reach her goal more readily. Pandit Rajmani Tigunait documents some of these sites, "The spiritual energy of Banaras, for example, is characterized by knowledge...at Ayodhya, by self-sacrifice...at Kamakhya, siddhis (supernatural powers), and at the site of 64 Yoginis (in Khajuraho), the spiritual energy of Khajuraho enables us to experience our body as a living shrine."

Georg Feuerstein in his book, "Tantra: The Path of Ecstasy", identifies the number 64 with Tantric implications, "as meaningful and sacred to Tantra as the number 108 to the Hindu traditions". He further argues that the number corresponds to the 64 Tantras, the 64 Bhairavas (forms of Shiva) and 64 Kalas (aspects of the Supreme Goddess), as mentioned in certain Tantric texts. Pandit Tigunait also observes, "In the Tantric tradition, the 64 yoginis are the presiding deities that guide and govern the entire fabric of life. They not only hold the body and mind together, but also animate them (prana). Awakening these forces is the essence of spiritual accomplishments."

Erotic Motifs

While there exist multiple explanations for the profusion of erotic imagery in Khajuraho, an attempt can be made to bring some of the most plausible ones to the foreground. With the gradual intensification of feudalism in India, local interests and polities strengthened. Regionalism strongly influenced art forms, and eroticism, an integral part of life, got canonized in art.

In the essay 'Sexual Imagery on the Phantasmagorical Castles at Khajuraho', published in the International Journal of Tantric Studies (November 1996), Michael Rabe attributes the erotic imagery to protection. Rabe cites a passage from the Zilpa Prakaza (a contemporary text): "the Naribandha (frieze of a woman) is indispensable in architecture. As a house without a wife, as frolic without a woman, so without (the figure of) a woman, the monument will be of inferior quality. A place without love-images is in the opinion of Kaulacaras (Tantric authorities) always a base, forsaken place, a dark abyss".

Whether the Chandella dynasty was motivated by Tantra is unknown, but the belief that Tantra was known in the 9th to 12th centuries finds evidence. Rabe pursues that the famed maithuna couplings stand eloquent testimony to the 'left hand' path of Tantra, the Vamamarga—they embody the principle of 'the yoga of bhoga.' The Tantric tradition frequently juxtaposes yoga (disciplined action) and bhoga (pleasure), underlining a complex integration.

Taking the argument further, Georg Feuerstein ponders that the Tantrik neither neurotically embrace sensory pleasures (bhoga), nor do they crave for mystical union (yoga). For them, women are Shakti; sex is the love play between Shiva and Shakti, and pleasure is a modification of supreme bliss. Vijnana Bhairava Tantra (a Tantric text) also explains that it is the mind that is the real cause of bondage or liberation. For those pure in mind, everything is pure. For those whose mind is defiled with misconceptions and base emotions, even the pure is polluted.

Chausathi Yoginis and their Vahanas

The Chausathi Yoginis are carved as standing on their vahanas, ready to move and perform their tasks. The differences in the type of vahanas chosen by each yogini, again highlight the importance of difference and indicate how distinction in terms of work was significant during those times when women did not have a guide book of feminism to advise them of the pursuits to follow and dreams to cherish.

1. Maya/ Bahurupa/ Chandika – stands on a corpse lying straight
2. Tara – stands on a corpse
3. Narmada – stands on an elephant
4. Yamuna – stands on a tortoise
5. Shanti/ Kanti/ Laxmi/ Manada – stands on a full blown lotus
6. Vriddhi/ Kriya/ Varuni – Lines of waves on the pedestal
7. Gauri/ Ksemankari – stands on an alligator
8. Aindri/ Indrani- stands on an elephant
9. Varahi – boar faced, stands on a buffalo
10. Ranavira/ Padmavati – stands on a snake
11. Ostraarudha/ Vanarmukhi – monkey faced, stands on a camel

12. Vaishnavi – Grauda is her mount
13. Kalaratri/ Panchavarahi – stands on a boar
14. Vadyaroopa – stands on a drum
15. Charchika – stands on a demon
16. Marjari/ Betali – stands on a fish
17. Chinnamastaka – stands on a severed human head
18. Vrisabhanana/ Bindhya Basini – stands on mountains
19. Jalakamini – stands on a frog
20. Ghatavara – stands on a lion, lifting an elephant over her head
21. Vikarali/ Kakarali – stands on a dog
22. Saraswati – stands on a serpent
23. Birupa – the pedestal she stands on has lines of waves
24. Kauveri – stands on 7 ratna kalasas on full blown lotus
25. Varahi/ Bhalluka – there is a padma lata on her pedestal
26. Narasimhi/ Simhamukhi – Lion faced, stands on a pedestal with 5 flowers and leaves
27. Biraja – stands on a lotus bud with leaves
28. Vikatanana – protuding lips and curling matted hair, the pedestal with mount is broken
29. Mohalaxmi – stands on a full bloom open lotus
30. Kaumari – stands on a peacock
31. Mahamaya – She is worshiped as the presiding deity of the temple.
32. Usa/ Rati – stands on a pedestal with an archer with a bow in his hands (Kandrap or cupid)
33. Karkari – stands on a crab
34. Sarpashya/ Chittala – Snake faced, the mount is broken
35. Yasha – the mount is a pedestal with 4 legs
36. Aghora/ Vaivasvati– stands on a horned goat like animal
37. Bhadrakali/ Rudrakali – stands on a crow

38. Matangi/ Shitala/ Vainayaki/ Ganeshani/ Gajanana – stands on a donkey
39. Bhindhyabalini – stands on a rat
40. Abhya/ Veera Kumari – stands on a scorpion
41. Maheshwari – stands on a bull
42. Kamakshi/ Ambika – stands on a mongoose
43. Kamayani – stands on a cock
44. Ghatabari – stands on a lion
45. Stutee – stands on a haladi kathua
46. Kali – stands on a recumbent male figure
47. Uma – stands on pedestal of lotus flowers
48. Narayani – stands on a pedestal with a conical pot with a lid
49. Samudra – stands on a pedestal with a conch shell
50. Brahmani – 3 faces, stands on a book
51. Jwalamukhi – stands on a platform with 8 legs
52. Agneyi – stands on a ram with flames of fire in the background
53. Aditi – stands on a parrot
54. Chandrakanti – stands on a cot with 4 legs
55. Vayubega – stahds on a female yak
56. Chamunda – stands on a musk deer, with a lion over her head
57. Murati – stands on a deer
58. Ganga – stands on a 'makara'
59. Dhumavati/ Tarini – stands on a goose with a winnower in her hand
60. Gandhari – stands on a donkey
61. Surva Mangala – the niche is empty but it is believed to be Surva Mangala
62. Ajita – stands on a stag
63. Surya Putri – stands on a galloping horse
64. Vayu Veena – stands on a black buck

Evolution of the Shakti Cult in Odisha

The worship of Mother Goddess or Shakti, can be traced back to the Pre-Vedic or Indus Valley Civilisation. Devisukta of the Rig Veda is the primary source of the Shakti Cult. In the Rig Veda there is a description of a goddess named 'Aditi'. She is depicted not only as Mother Goddess but also as an emblem of the divine spirit. But it is difficult to ascertain when this cult made its first appearance in ancient Odisha. However, from the epigraphic and iconographic stand-point, it is obvious that the evolution of Shakti Cult in Odisha is not prior to the 4th century AD. The earliest epigraphic evidence regarding the Shakti worship in Odisha is found in a Copper-Plate Grant of Tushtikara Deva, who perhaps flourished about the 5th or 6th Century AD and was a worshipper of goddess Stambhesvari. There is a pillar of Stambhesvari at Sonepur and a temple of the goddess at Aska in Ganjam. We have reference to that deity in the Grants of Sulki and Bhanja kings. We are also inclined to take Stambhesvari as another form of Khambesvari, the popular deity among the aboriginal people of some areas of ex-feudatary States of Odisha. The primitive tribes even today, set up a big piece of stone or a piece of wood with eyes, mouth painted crudely with indigenous colours, usually under a tree in some central place or outside the village and worship it as the guardian-deity of the village.

Jajpur, on the bank of river Vaitarani, is an old and prominent seat of Shakti Cult and tantric worship, and its history goes back to the days of the Mahabharata when it was considered a sacred place of pilgrimage. The image of Viraja, now worshipped in the temple at Jajpur, is a two-handed Mahisasuramardini, engaged in killing a buffalo-demon. As the image of Mahisasuramardini depicted on the Gupta temple of Bhumara is four-handed, it is maintained that the present image of Viraja in the temple of Jajpur belongs to the 5th Century AD It was during the early Bhaumakara rule in Odisha that the Durga image became eight-armed (Asthabhuja) and during the later Bhaumakara period, this image is found to be ten-armed (Dashabhuja). The popularity of Shakti worship at Jajpur is born out of the fact that the Bhaumakara queen Tribhuban Mahadevi compared hereself with Katyayini (Durga or Viraja) at her accession. During the Sailadbhaba and Bhaumakara periods, Tantricism grew from 7th Century AD The Tantriks worshipped the Mother Goddess as the source of power or shakti and the origin of the highest spiritual bliss. From 7th century onwards Tantricism continued to dominate Buddhism, Shaivism and Brahmanical religions. The great Shaiva centre of Bhubaneswar has also a number of Shakta temples built during the Bhauma period. The most ancient Shakti shrine of Bhubaneswar is the temple of Vaitala and its sculpture clearly proves that the strange esoteric rites were being performed in it. Four Shakta shrines sprang up on the four sides of Bindu Sarobara near the Lingaraj temple and they are now known as Vaitala, Mohini, Uttareswar temples. The name of the Shakta shrine on the east of the tank, which still exists, has been lost. These Shakta shrines contain either the images of Chamunda or of Mahisasuramardini. Among them, the Vaitala is the most prominent and a study of its sculpture and architecture indicates that the strange esoteric rites including human sacrifice, were being performed in it. The presiding deity of Vaitala temple is goddess Chamunda garlanded with skulls and she is of terrific form and is known as Kapalini. This Kapalini was the deity of the Kapalikas. Besides the Vaitala temple, Kichakeswari (Chamunda) is also the presiding deity of the largest temple at Khiching in the Mayurbhanj district which is the creation of the Bhauma age. The worship of Sapta Matruka (seven - Mothers) was another form of Saktism during the Bhaumakara period. The seven goddesses are Varahi, Indrani, Vaishnavi, Kaumari, Sivani, Brahmani and Chamunda. The deities are two or four-armed. The earliest representations of such matrukas was found at Parasurameswar, Vaitala and Mukteswar temples at Bhubaneswar. The Sapta Matruka images have also been found at Jajpur, Belhandi in the Kalahandi district, Markendeswar tank at Puri, Salanpur in Jagatsinghpur etc. These Seven Mothers are accompanied by Ganesha and Virabhadra. The iconographic peculiarity divides the Matrukas of Odisha into two broad groups, earlier and later.

With the rise of Tantric Buddhism and Tantric Saivism during the Bhaumakara period, Yogini worship became popular in Odisha prior to the 10th Century AD The Kalika

Purana mentions 'Odra' as one of the important Brahmanical tantric pithas of India. The temple of Hirapur, which stands not far from the south bank of the river Bhargavi was first discovered by Sri K. N. Mohapatra in the year 1953. There is a similar temple of Yogini at Ranipur Jharial in the Titlagarh sub-division of Bolangir district. The dimension of this pitha is bigger than that of Hirapur. During the Somavamsi rule, Shaktism gained momentum in Odisha.

Thus, evolution of Shakti cult, through the centuries, indicates that worship of the Mother Goddess in various forms continued unperturbed. There are numerous Shakti shrines in Odisha of which the shrines of Viraja at Jajpur, Samaleswari at Sambalpur, Bhagabati at Banpur, Mangala at Kakatpur, Charchika at Banki, Sarala at Jhankada, Kichakeswari at Khiching are most famous. (Ref:Balabhadra Ghadai)

Literature on Tantra, mythology and iconography of Yoginis in Odisha

There are accounts of nearly one thousand palm-leaf manuscripts among other valuable palm-leaf manuscripts available in the collection of the Odisha State museum at Bhubaneswar. These manuscripts focus on Tantra or Mantra Shastra, which constitute an important branch of both the Buddhistic and Brahmanical religious and ritualistic traditions. The collection describe the changing tantric rituals now current in Odisha. The script used in the manuscripts is generally Odia but the language is either Sanskrit or Odia. There are few manuscripts in Bengali and Nagari scripts also. The manuscripts are written on palm leaf which was easily available. The rarity of palm leaf manuscripts was noticed in 1876.

The famous commentator Kulluka Bhatta asserts that there are only two kinds of Shrutis, namely Vaidika and Tantrika. Tantra is also widely regarded as the scriptural authority for the present age - the Kaliyuga. On that account, it is sometimes classified as the fifth Veda. But in a restricted sense, Tantra denotes a religious system connected with Shakti worship having its own doctrinal theories.

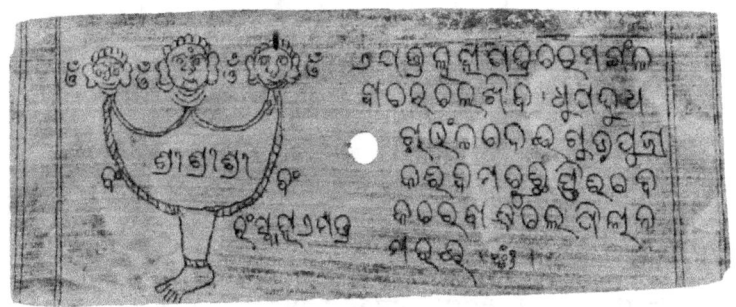

Palm leaf inscriptions of Tantra

Saptamatrika

The earliest existing temple dedicated to the worship of Durga is found on the top of a small hill near Patiakila, which may definitely be assigned to the Gupta period. Here the deity is carved in a single stone, which also forms the back wall of the temple.

The religious history of Odisha is unique in that it is cosmopolitan in nature. Here all the Pancha Devatas, namely Vishnu, Shiva, Surya, Ganapati and Shakti are worshipped in their traditional pithas in Puri, Bhubaneswar, Konark, Mahavinayaka and Jajpur. The earliest epigraphic evidence regarding Shakti worship in Odisha is found in a copper-plate grant of Tushtikara Deva who perhaps flourished in 5th or 6th century AD and was a worshipper of goddess Stambhesvari. Dr. D. C. Sarkar states that Stambhesvari was the family deity of the Shulkis and was represented in the form of a pillar indicating Shiva and Shakti. The same goddess is also mentioned in the copperplate inscriptions of the Bhanjas and the Tungas who ruled over different parts of Odisha from the 8th to the 11th century AD There is a pillar of Stambesvari at Sonepur and a temple of the goddess at

Aska in Ganjam. The practice of worshipping wodden pillars continues in many villages of the hill tribes, who worship this Goddess with wine and meat, having Tantric affiliation.

Tantric Pithas in Odisha

Some of the early Tantras refer to four Pithas. This chatus pitha conception may have some relation with Chatuspitha Parvata near Jajpur in Odisha, the great Tantric centre. These four hills i. e. Udaygiri, Ratnagiri, Lalitgiri and Pushpagiri are regarded as representing the four great tantra pithas inside Odisha. Obviously, Odisha was a land of primary importance in the Tantric world, and out of these four pithas mentioned in the Tantric texts, two of them namely Oddiyana and Purnagiri may be located in Odisha.

Yogini Pithas in Odisha

The Yogini cult was prevalent prior to the 10th century AD References to Mahayoginis in Somadeva's "Yasatilaka" composed in 959 A. D support the prevalence of this cult prior to the 10th century AD

It is gathered from Tantra literature that the large number of pithas which were only four to start with, varied according to different versions and attained the maximum of one hundred and eighty which is a conventional figure.

Yoginis are Mother Goddesses who are worshipped at the beginning of every Sanskara. The Principal yoginis are seven or eight but their number is at times raised to sixty-four. The principal seven or eight called matrikas or Mother goddesses.

Temples celebrating the yogini cult are found at two places in Odisha, namely at Hirapur (near Bhubaneswar) and at Ranipur Jharial (Bolangir District). Shri V. Karambelkar has discussed in his paper "Matsyendranath and his Yogini Cult" about a Yogini temple situated at Suruda or Sorada, a place in the South Odisha

Tantricism held its sway over the people of Odisha at least from the beginning of the seventh century AD which marks the decline of traditional Buddhism. Many Puranas, Tantras and religious codes dealing with Tantric philosophy were composed or complied during this period in India. When worship of Shakti was popular in India, as well as in Odisha, many Shakta temples were built, the presiding deities of which were Shaktis in their various forms. There are many temples in Odisha where the Devi or the presiding deity is worshipped according to Shakta rituals.

Two manuscripts namely Durgayajana Dipika & Tarinikula Sudha Tarangini elucidate that Tantricism not only held it's sway over the people of Odisha from the beginning of the seventh century AD but continued for a

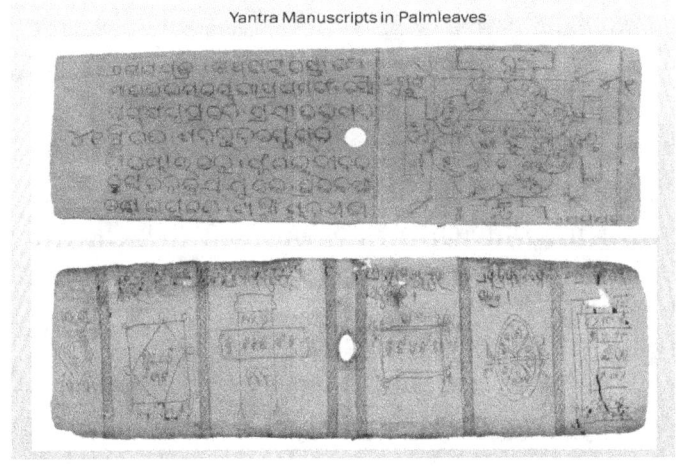

Yantra Manuscripts in Palmleaves

reasonably long period and there were Odia Tantrikas who popularised Tantra by composing Tantric texts.

Durgayajana Dipika was written by Jagannatha Acharya, an Odia Tantrik of the 18th Century. This is a palm-leaf manuscript of the size 15. 4" X 1. 3" and contains one hundred thirty folios in Odia character and was copied by Shri Maguni Charana Mohapatra. The language of the Manuscript is Sanskrit, but the language is corrupt at

Some tantric Illustrations in Palmleaf Manuscripts

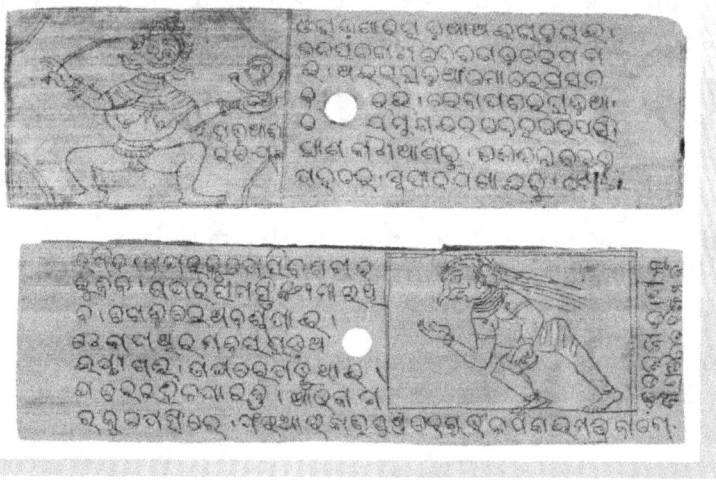

places. There are usually five lines of writing to a page and the manuscript is in a good state of preservation.

Mythologically, the Yoginis have different stories of origin. The first story of origin is that the Yoginis have all evolved from different parts of the Devi's body. Each Yogini is said to have emerged from parts of the Devi, like her naval, sweat, voice, arms, and anger. This story is the Shakti and Tantric adaptation of the Chandi Purana (15th Century AD), where the 64 Yoginis each represent a specific aspect of Devi, the Mother Goddess – whether it may be her anger or her cunning nature, which, together represent the entirety of her power, show how they all stand for the destruction of delusions and liberation through spiritual insight. (Tiwari, S. K. "Yoginis and Matrikas". Tribal Roots of Hinduism2015).

A different version of the same story is that these Yoginis are attendants of the Devi, the Mother Goddess, which is explained Agni Purana (10th Century AD), where they are referred to as the "Attributes of the Goddess". In the text, they were concerned with the welfare of the villages and the practices of the people. Because of the connection with Devi and Tantric influences, they are credited with having a connection to the good and bad world of spirits, which also explains why shamans of those times were called 'yogic'. (Tate, Karen. "The Asian Sub Continent". Sacred Places of Goddess: 108 Destinations).

Iconographically, the Yoginis are portrayed in therianthropomorphic form: human body with animal heads. Although there are 64 Yoginis, each Yogini has specific attributes unique to herself. However, in general, depicted with voluptuous bodies and fierce faces, they have multiple arms where they carry human bones and arms and legs as ornaments. Adorned in human and animal skin for clothes, some Yoginis even wear garlands made out of skulls or rotting human heads. Common objects held are weapons like a long pole while some carry rosary to show their patronage to Devi. (Abbasi, A. A., and S. K. Tiwari. "Zoomorphic Forms". Dimensions of Human Cultures in Central India: Professor S. K. Tiwari)

Mother goddess worship or the cult of the mother goddess has its roots deeply embedded in the religious settings of the sub-continent. The roots of this cult can be traced back to the Indus Valley Civilization and the early Chalcolithic terracotta mother goddess figurines from the pre-Harappan period. This cult gained in popularity in the Mauryan and Sunga-Kushana periods.

The literary developments in the subsequent Gupta period added much value to such worship and/or concepts, thus reinforced the strong textual traditions which support such rituals and religious activities. These texts include the Devibhagvat, Skandapurana, Kalikapurana, Chaturvargiya chintamani and Brihadsamvita.

These religious cults developed in accordance with their times and were further divided into multiple branches. The mother goddess cult was widespread. From these varied practices Shakti as a concept gained the attention of people leading to the creation of myriad Shakta pithas. These then became a place or platform to perform rituals related to the various goddesses.

Amongst these the most enigmatic and dramatic was the rise of the cult of the Chausath-yoginis. The essential concept of syncretic Shakta worship is beautifully interpreted into the religious symbolism and iconic perception of the female generic yoni. The yoni in its turn is incomplete and inseparable from the linga. In its iconic form the linga is represented by Shiva, most often in his avatarsRudra and Bhairava. Together the 'goddess/yogini and Shiva' and the 'yoni and linga' represent the coming together of 'Purusa and Prakriti' thus completing the cosmic whole. Bhairava is the god who balances andstands as the crucial male principle of Shakta spiritual ideology and practices thus symbolising the masculine element of the Shakta tantric sects. Texts like Devi Bhagwat, Markendeya

Purana, Kalika Purana etc. shed light on this element of Bhairava.

According to the Kalika Purana the one male god associated with the Yoginis is Bhairava -popularly known as 'Lord of Yogini(s)'. This is perhaps the first clue in understanding the complex relationship between Yogini and Bhairava. Here the confusion or question is who follows who?

The Yogini(s) and Bhairava(s) have very similar functions and identity clashes i. e. both have 64 forms, both are often related to cremation grounds or death, both are given similar propitiatory offerings during rituals, temples of both deities are situated outside the habitation areas or villages, both practice 'tantric' rituals, both have strong affiliations with folk/local traditions, both have individual identities in classical aesthetics, both have independent positions in the religious setting as well as the social setting.

Chausathi Yoginis of Hirapur and the Yoginis of Angkor Wat

The thinkers of ancient India interpreted the temple as the reclining body of a woman with her womb symbolizing the sanctum sanctorum of the enshrined deity. Temples were sculptural and architectural celebrations of sensuality and fertility that was in direct contradiction of the strict, monastic sterility of Buddhist viharas. A thousand years ago, before the construction of the grand temple complexes of India dedicated to male deities such as Vishnu and Shiva, before the advent of Islam that celebrated a formless God, India had temples exclusively dedicated to womanhood — the circular temples of the yoginis.

Few still survive. These temples were abandoned long ago for mysterious reasons. Was it a natural decline following rise of devotional cults to Shiva and Vishnu? Was it the opposition by Vedantic monasticism led by celibate men? Was it the arrival of Muslim warlords such as the Afghan general Kalapahada who attacked Odisha and destroyed much of its iconography? One can only speculate and wonder. The temples were rediscovered and restored by archaeologists only in the last century. Sanskrit texts are ambiguous about these deities, with numerous lists of names, and attributes, and rituals, but no binding mythology other than tales of Durga and Kali riding out to battle with armies of female warriors, often the shaktis of male gods, who drink the blood of asuras.

The images in Hirapur show women in various postures. Some dancing, some hunting with bows and tridents, some making music on drums, some drinking blood or wine, some doing household chores. Most women are bejewelled, with fine hairstyles. Others have the head of a snake, or a bear, or a lion, or an elephant. They stand on human heads, male bodies, on crows, roosters, peacocks, bulls, buffaloes, donkeys, pigs, scorpions, crabs, camels, dogs, on water and in the midst of fire. Some are recognisable — like the gaunt Chamunda, the lute-bearing Saraswati, the pot-holding Lakshmi, female forms of Vishnu's avatars such as Narasimhi and Varahi and of Vedic gods like Indrani.

What is clear is that yoginis are life-affirming. If the yogi withdrew from life, the yoginis seemed to have embraced life. If the yogi yearned for immortality, the yogini did not fear mortality. If the yogi sought to withhold desires, the yogini unleashed desires.

All these circular shrines have a central structure. At Hirapur, the central structure is a pavilion, empty and opens to the sky, with four Bhairava and four Yogini images on the four walls. At Ranipur, the central shrine is occupied by a three headed image of Bhairava, Shiva's fierce form. At Morena, there is the linga. At Bhedaghat, there is a temple that enshrines, rather unusually, the image of Shiva and Parvati on Nandi. Was it placed there later? For Shiva temples typically worship Shiva in aniconic form (linga) rather than iconic form (svarupa).

When the goddess appears as a collective in Tantrik traditions, even when they stand in a line and not in a circle, they are accompanied by one male — the Bhairava, often shown as fierce and with an erect phallus. He accompanies them, as guardian and lover. The women circle him.

Angkor Wat, the famous 12th century Hindu temple now located amidst the dense forests of Cambodia, is the largest religious structure in the world. This Khmer temple has for nearly 1000 years, enshrined the images of more than 1,796 sacred women.

'Angkor' as it is known world-wide is what was once the capital city of the Khmer Empire that existed in Cambodia between the 9th and 12th centuries CE. The temple ruins in the area of Siem Reap are the colossal remnants of the Angkorian capital, and are indicative of the pinnacle at which the ancient Khmer architecture, art and civilization had prevailed.

The inscriptions of the images of goddesses on the walls, nooks and corners of Angkor has been a topic of considerable debate. There is not much information available on who these women of Angkor Wat were and what principles of spirituality they represent.

Each female portrait at Angkor Wat is distinctly different, with unique varieties in their pose, hand positions (mudras), ethnicity, jewellery, clothing, hair style, accoutrements and location. (Kent Davis)Similarly, the Chausath Yoginis of Hirapur are all unique in their stance, the mounts, intricate jewellery and particularly, the elaborate coiffure. Indian Yogini traditions involve both female worshipers and female divinities. It is unknown if the Khmer religion at the time of Angkor Wat had similar female-centric traditions. However, it is quite clear that Khmer temples prominently featured sacred women to the near exclusion of men. A handful of Indian Yogini temples exhibit this same trait. (Davis)

Can the Angkor goddesses be categorized as Yoginis? Most of the Angkor images are gentler than the Yogini statues at Hirapur. They appear more reserved in their appearance and seem to reflect only the gentler aspects of the Yogini pantheon. A very interesting observation is that the images of women at Angkor Wat display no ferocious or supernatural aspect. In fact, they appear quite normal, lacking fangs, halos, wings or other fantastic features.

Angkor Wat devata from the bakkan, the sacred level of the temple. Photo: Kent Dav

No woman at Angkor Wat appears as a sakti, the manifestation of the female aspect of a god, sometimes seen with the animal head of a boar, bull, horse or lion like at Chausath Yogini temple. Nor do the Angkor Wat women possess necklaces made from human skulls, skeletons or weapons among their accouterments. All of the devata at Angkor Wat are standing in dignified poses with both feet firmly on the ground. None are seated. Only a few assume kinetic positions that can be associated with dance. (Davis)

However, despite the obvious dissimilarities, the women of Angkor Wat do share a divine connection with their Yogini sisters. Some also display similar hand positions (mudras), jewelry adornments and an association with plants and flowers from nature.

Apsaras are popular motifs in the stone bas-reliefs of the Angkorian temples in Cambodia. In harmony with the Indian connection of dance with apsaras, Khmer female figures that are dancing are regarded as apsaras; female figures, depicted individually or in groups, who are standing still and facing forward in the manner of temple guardians or custodians are called devatas.

Apsara dance, 12th century Bayon temple, Angkor Wat

Angkor Wat, the largest Angkorian temple (built AD 1116–1150), features both apsaras and devata; however the devata type are the most numerous with more than 1,796 in the present research inventory. Angkor Wat architects used small apsara images as decorative motifs on pillars and walls. They incorporated larger devata images (full-body portraits measuring approximately 95–110 cm) more prominently at every level of the temple from the entry pavilion to the tops of the high towers. In 1927, Sappho Marchal published a study cataloging the remarkable diversity of their hair, headdresses, garments, stance, jewelry and decorative flowers, which Marchal concluded were based on actual practices of the Angkor period.

Sacredness And Spirituality

Yogini Narmada, Chausathi Yogini temple, Hirapur

Introduction:
In the ever-expanding tourism market, undoubtedly tourism and culture are inter-related and are major drivers of destination attractiveness and competitiveness. An attempt has been made to analyze how the combination of sacredness and spirituality could help position Chausath Yogini temple situated at Hirapur as a cultural-heritage

destination of importance. At a time when modernity is pushing people into a chaotic identity-crisis, the cultural heritage strengthens cultural and historical identity. Despite its historic, cultural and architectural grandeur, Chausath Yogini temple lies in relative anonymity and requires aggressive promotion. There are significant components of sacredness and spirituality at Chausath Yogini temple which continue to fascinate the discerning reader.

Numerical grouping of Yoginis:

"The numerical groupings associated with the Yoginis show variance from text to text, but the most common grouping is sixty-four There are very few references to yoginis being alone. The numbers eight, twelve, sixteen and sixty-four seem to elevate the yoginis to a higher status" (Donaldson). The number eight is considered to be very auspicious and has great potency within the Hindu religion (Dehejia). As the square of eight, sixty-four, has even more power and is considered to be extremely auspicious in Tantric literature When the Yoginis are divided into groups of eight, it is, usually, to associate each group with a separate deity. The groups usually take on the attributes of whichever deity they are connected with. Although the grouping of the yoginis into sixty-four is fairly uniform throughout the literature, their names, descriptions and characteristics are not (Donaldson).

The Yogini

The yoginis have been classified in different texts according to the functions, names and rituals attached to them. (Origin of Tantricism and Sixty-Four Yogini Cult in Orissa -- Dr. Janmejay Choudhury)

Categories:
- The Yoginis are sixty-four in number and are classified as Sahaja, Kulaja and Antyeja.
- Another text divides yoginis into Ksetraja, Pithaja, Yogaja and Mantraja based on different principles. The first two groups of the second classification have association with the sacred pithas; the yogajas are propitiated with yogic practices and the mantrajas with Mantras. The mother goddesses such as Brahmani, Maheswari, Vaisnavi, Indrani etc. are classified as yoginis.
- The yogini kaula of Matsyendranath also refers to the worship of mystic circles made up of 4, 8, 12, 64 and more angles at the centre of which there is Siva, omnipresent, immovable and un-dualified. The sixty-four yoginis are most probably so many angles representing the equal number of manifestations of the Shakti embracing Siva. The circle thus forms a 'Lotus', reminder of the famous Tantric Srichakra. This theory of Matsyendra holds good when the extant yogini temples are taken into consideration. Various sources have furnished different numbers of yoginis, but ultimately the number sixty-four appears to have been accepted by all the authorities.
- Of these sixty-four yoginis, the principal seven or eight are known as mother goddesses such as Brahmani, Maheswari, Vaisnavi, Kaumari, Varabi, Indrani and Chamunda, who according to the Puranic stories were created to drink blood of the demons. It is probable that these eight principal mother goddesses who are evidently the yoginis were multiplied into sixty-four.
- That the cult of sixty-four yoginis was widely prevalent

is evident from several lists of sixty-four yoginis recorded in different texts. The Kalika purana, Skanda purana, Brihadnandikeswara Purana, Cansatha yogini namavali, Chandi purana of Sarala Das, Durgapuja, Brihndla Tantra, Bata Avakasa of Balaram Das and other texts contain lists of sixty-four yoginis.
- Another list enumerates as many as sixty-nine yoginis in eight categories.
- Sixty-four yoginis are associated with sixty-four kalas, sixty-four Ratibandhas, sixty-four Bhairavas, sixty-four Nayikas and sixty-four emotions of human-being.
- In Hirapur Yogini temple the images are all associated with their Vahanas, whereas at Ranipur Jharial they are in dancing poses. The images of Bhedaghat temple of Madhya Pradesh are seated in Lalitasana.
- In one of the religious traditions of India, there are 8 major forms of Devi, the Goddess. These are known as the Ashta Matrikas (8 Mothers). Each of these has 8 attendants and so we arrive at the number, 64. Each of the 64 can be further correlated to the currents or winds of the human "etheric" body, or viewed as a type of neurotic or unproductive tendency (if not balanced by the others). However, these Matrikas, or other aspects of Devi such as the fearsome Chamundas, do not appear at the Hirapur temple. (www.khandro.net)
- By meditating on each of the 64 petals we can induce the resident yogini to grant a boon in the form of a siddhi (special ability). The Kaula tradition teaches that in the 64-fold complex of matrices lie all the secrets of bodily perfection and also, of alchemy.

Though the leaders of the modern Yoga-asana & meditation traditions have often been males, the vast majority of modern practitioners are female, (Gates, Janice. Yogini: The Power of Woman, 2006, Mandala Publishing) including many who have attained mastery via steadfast awareness through the Shakti sensations of fertility, childbirth, and other rites of passage. In the Shakta branch of Hinduism, creation myths place the Divine Feminine at their center, taking the Tantric view that the nature of the Cosmos (or Macrocosm) is reflected in the human body (or Microcosm), and it is the Female who gestates and gives birth to new life. "Only the female can awaken the muladhara chakra (the seat of the Kundalini-shakti) via fertility and sexuality; the male must use kriya Yoga". (Dr Swami Shankardevananda Saraswati, "The Importance of Shakti", YOGA Magazine, May 1999 London, England)

Sacredscapes:
- **A Hypaethral Temple:** The Chausath Yogini temple is unique in being one of the few Hypaethral Temples of the world. Origin of hypaethral Latin hypaethrus exposed to the open air, (from Greek hypaithros, from hypo- + aitherether, air). It was described by the Roman architect

Chausathi Yogini temple, Hirapur

Vitruvius in his treatise "On Architecture" written for the emperor Caesar Augustus probably about 15 BC.

What is the essential sacred element of a hypaethral temple? A study of history reveals that the innermost sanctuary of some ancient temples (In the Israelite tradition known as the Holy of Holies) was sometimes open to the sky, hyp-aethral, or "under heaven. " This can most likely be attributed to the temple's design to match the cosmos. Examples can be found in Stonehenge and Göbekli Tepe. Temples, the world over have often been closely tied with the cosmos, adorned with cosmological symbols. The fact that some ancient temples also seem to have been hypaethral, or open to the sky, is evidence enough to postulate that it was to facilitate cosmological observation and veneration. 64 Joginis Temple is a tantric temple, with hypaethral architecture as tantric prayer rituals involve worshiping the bhumandala (environment consisting all the 5 elements of nature - fire, water, earth, sky and ether).

- **The sacred number 64**

The symbol of number 64 is a product of 8 directions and replication of each one in the asthamandala/ asthaka-cakra (eight points on the cosmic circuit). This theoretic or esoteric interpretation is explained in the Agni Purana, AgP (52; 146) that prescribes that one goddess must preside over each group of the 8 goddesses. The primordial number of eight matrikas (mother goddesses) symbolises the condensation (sankocha) of the cosmic rhythm, and the number 64, resulting to the emergence of the matri-chakra or matrimandala represent its expansion (purna vikas). This pattern is clear by the geometrical arrangement of the 64 Yoginis. Thus, the number eight and sixty-four are the two phases of creation. Following the framework of the AgP,4, the placement of 64 Yoginis would be arranged into an Eight-petal (lotus) Yantra where each petal places eight forms of Yogini. Each of the petals is ascribed to a specific direction; and each direction is under the control of one of the eight forms of Matrikas : Brahmi (east), Maheshvari (southeast), Kaumari (south), Vaishnavi (southwest), Varahi (west), Aindri (northwest), Camunda (north), and Narasimhi (northeast).

(Cosmic Order and Cultural Astronomy: Sacred Cities of India: Goddesses and Spatial Ordering in Kashi: Rana P. B. Singh, Cambridge Scholars Publishing,2009)

- One of the most interesting and unique sculptures found here is that of "Ekapada Shiva" or the one legged Shiva. He is also known as Ajaikapada Bhairava. There are only two references to the presence of such a form, one in Odisha and the other at Shore temple, Mahabalipuram.

- Other interesting features around this temple are that every male deity except Shiva are replaced by a female counterpart including Ganesha. The temple also hosts forms of Bhairava and Chamunda, who are better known as the fierce forms of Shiva and Kali.

Yogini Chakra

The Chakra or Circle as a whole is a symbol so simple and pure in form and concept that it has been used as a symbol or Bimba or imagery from times immemorial to avant garde creativity. The circle represents the sun, eye, time, zodiac such a form and shape which represents a complimentary concept of competitiveness and separateness.

The circle is complex in itself without any beginning or end and separates everything outside itself. The circle is also a symbol of self, mentions. Vidya Dehejia in her magnum opus publication "Yogini cult and temples - a tantric tradition". It is a self contained psyche in all aspects. Literature that refers to the yoginis invariably speak of them as forming a chakra or brunda, both meaning circle.

Chakra pujas, were performed in Yogini temples. No comprehensive training and experience of Kaula Marg Tantra could be complete without participation in the chakra puja. This is the most classical form of group sadhana in tantra. Chakras often refer to the vortexes of energy in our subtle bodies. In Tantra, the chakra puja is also used as a tool for inner realization and empowerment. Chakra puja also refers to a circle formed by Tantric couples who utilize the vortex of energy created by the closed circumference to enhance the power of their practice. The circle represents the zodiac, the all-seeing eye, time, and energy itself. It is the ultimate symbol of the inmost self. The Chakra puja focussed on the physical plane to transcend the physical plane.

However the Chakra puja's were opposed by orthodox Hindus. While the vast bulk of Tantric literature relating to the chakra puja has been written over the most recent millennium, references to chakra pujas can be found in much earlier texts. Sage Kalhana is said to have made numerous references to yogini chakras nearly 2000 years ago in his Rajatarangini Manuscript.

Tantrik Worship: In Yogini worship, the Tantrik symbol is a chakra with 64 spokes in the wheel. Each spoke represents a Yogini form of Mother Devi. In the Buddhist Kalachakra tantric system, the navel chakra or the Wheel of Emanation, the 64 channels are the 64 goddesses of the Speech Mandala. In Kaula Marga Tantric system, eight chakras or lotus with eight petals each was taught by Matsyendranath.

The Mandala

A mandala (circle) is a spiritual and ritual symbol in Indian religions, representing the universe. [Webster online dictionary] In common parlance, "mandala" has become a generic term for a diagram, chart or geometric pattern that symbolizes the cosmos metaphysically or symbolically; a microcosm of the universe.

The basic form of most mandalas is a square with four gates containing a circle with a center point. Each gate is in the general shape of a T. (Artiste Nomade, What's a mandala?) Mandalas often exhibit radial balance. In various spiritual traditions, mandalas may be used as a spiritual guidance tool, for establishing a sacred space, and as an aid to meditation and trance induction.

According to art therapist and mental health counselor Susanne F. Fincher, we owe the re-introduction of mandalas into modern Western thought to Carl Jung, the Swiss psychoanalyst. In his pioneering exploration of the unconscious through his own art making, Jung observed the motif of the circle spontaneously appearing. The circle drawings reflected his inner state at that moment. Familiarity with the philosophical writings of India prompted Jung to adopt the word "mandala" to describe these circle drawings he and his patients made. In his autobiography, Jung wrote:

I sketched every morning in a notebook a small circular drawing, which seemed to correspond to my inner situation at the time. . . . Only gradually did I discover what the mandala really is: . . . the Self, the wholeness of the personality, which if all goes well is harmonious.
— Carl Jung, Memories, Dreams, Reflections, pp. 195 – 196.

Jung recognized that the urge to make mandalas emerges during moments of intense personal growth. Their appearance indicates a profound re-balancing process is underway in the psyche. The result of the process is a more complex and better integrated personality.

The mandala serves a conservative purpose—namely, to restore a previously existing order. But it also serves the creative purpose of giving expression and form to something that does not yet exist, something new and unique. . . . The process is that of the ascending spiral, which grows upward while simultaneously returning again and again to the same point.
—Jungian analyst Marie-Louise von Franz, C. G. Jung: Man and His Symbols, p. 225
(https://en. wikipedia. org/wiki/Mandala)

The concept of the sacred and divine is synonymous with the tradition of the Chausath Yogini, and has been since the beginning of time. The Yogini cult is a mystical, magical, powerful amalgamation of sacredness and spirituality. To many faithful the Chausathi Yogini Temple represents the embodiment of an all- powerful Divine Female figure, as yogini statues employ the creative force of Shakti to work her will.

Cultural Re-awakening of the Chausathi Yoginis

Katyatani, outer wall of Chausathi Yogini temple, Hirapur

"In the beginning God was a woman, and from her womb she created all that is, thus she is all things and all things are her."(Karen Tate:"Sacred Places of Goddess")

The intricate manner in which culture is inter-woven into the way tourism is interpreted is universal. Tourism is a cultural concept and varies in construction, forms and change cross culturally. Tourist behaviour and motives reflect how individuals acquire values, beliefs, and behaviour patterns viewed as appropriate within a culture. People tend to develop culture-based beliefs, largely on the basis of stereotypes, reflected in prescribed roles.

An understanding of the sacred helps us in the realization that there are specifics of balance, order, and harmony in the natural world. Odisha is a land of mysterious indigenous communities. A pronounced sense of sacredness and spirituality characterizes them. The mystic cult of Odisha has had a great impact on its social life, literature, music, art and architecture.

There is an intricate culture-tourism relationship which can be comprehended by relating the 64 Yoginis of the Yogini cult and the changing status of the goddess to that of women in society vis-a-vis tourism. Chausath Yogini temple stands as an embodiment of the venerated, all powerful Divine female figure, the "Yogini". Anna Dallapicola maintains that the Yogini's symbolize," the forces of fertility, vegetation, illness, death, yoga, magic", all forces of Shakti. Shaw states that the term can mean a female practitioner of yoga, or ritual arts, a female being with magical powers, or a type of female deity.

"Sixty and four are the instruments of enjoyment that tempt the individual soul (jiva). Sixty and four are the divisions (kalas) within jiva; Sixty and four are the chambers of jiva's chakras; Sixty and four; where Shiva-Shakti reside. "(Thirumandiram).

The waves of modernism have washed away the ancient occupation of the village dwellers of Hirapur where this temple is situated. Neglected and unnoticed, this ancient jewel of sacredness lies behind a modern structure that has subsequently come up, as yet untapped as a tourist destination of undeniable significance. Hirapur exhibits a rare combination of cultural and heritage tourism potential.

Cultural tourism is a segment of the tourism industry that is growing at an unprecedented pace as the trend towards specialized travel takes precedence. This trend is evident in the rising volume of tourists who seek adventure, culture, history, archaeology and interaction with local people (Hollinshead, 2004). Cultural tourism is one of the most significant global tourism markets. Culture and creative industries are being used most frequently to promote and popularize destinations and enhance their competitiveness and attractiveness. The world over, destinations are now focused on developing their tangible and intangible cultural assets to ensure a comparative advantage in an increasingly competitive tourism marketplace, and to create a prominent local distinctiveness in the face of globalization. Cultural heritage tourism is also gaining immense popularity among the new-age travelers. The neo educated traveler breaks stereo-types and unravels his own travel needs and patterns.

In the ever-expanding tourism market, undoubtedly tourism and culture are inter-related and are major drivers of destination attractiveness and competitiveness. There is need of an analysis of the different facets of the relationship between tourism, culture and regional attractiveness, and the interventions which can be taken up to enhance the relationship, with specific reference to the Chausath Yogini temple situated at Hirapur.

From the perspective of tourism, specifically cultural tourism it is necessary

- To promote and position Chausath Yogini temple, Hirapur as a cultural/heritage destination of importance - Categorization as a stand-alone destination, part of a circuit and / or as a major attraction for special interest groups.
- To identify novel marketing strategies to tap the latent potential of the aforementioned destination.
- To analyse the changing status of the goddess to that of women in society vis-a vis tourism.

Definition of Terms

Cultural heritage:- The complex of monuments, buildings and archeological sites of outstanding universal value from the point of view of history, art or science.

Cultural tourism:- Cultural tourism is defined as visits by persons fromoutside the host community motivated wholly or in part by interest in the historical, artistic, scientific or lifestyle/heritage offerings of a community, region, group or institution (Silberberg, 1995).

- Cultural tourism is experiential tourism based on being involved in and stimulated by the performing arts, visual arts, and festivals. Heritage tourism, whether in the form of visiting preferred landscapes, historic sites, buildings or monuments, is also experiential tourismin the sense of seeking an encounter with nature or feeling part of the history of the place (Hall and Zeppel, 1990).

Heritage Tourism:- Heritage tourismis a broad field of specialty travel, based on nostalgia for the past and the desire to experience diverse cultural landscapes and forms. It includes travel to festivals and other cultural events, visit to sites and monuments, travel to study nature, folklore or art or pilgrimages (Zeppel and Hall, 1992).

The word "heritage" in its broader meaning is generally

associated with the word 'inheritance', that is, something transferred from one generation to another. Owing to its role as a carrier of historical values from the past, heritage is viewed as part of the cultural tradition of a society. The concept of 'tourism', on the other hand, is really a form of modern consciousness (Nuryanti, 1996).

Richards G. (1995), defined Cultural tourism as "the movement of persons to cultural attractions away from their normal place of residence with the intention to gather new information and experiences to satisfy their cultural needs". Richards stated that cultural tourism includes all movements of persons to specific cultural attractions such as heritage sites, artistic and cultural manifestations, arts and drama outside their usual place of residence. Silberberg T. (1995),defines cultural tourism as visits by persons from outside the host community motivated wholly or in part by interest in the historical, scientific, artistic or lifestyle/heritage offerings of a community, region, Group or institution'. WTO (1985) has provided a definition of cultural tourism, focusing on the travel motivations of tourists: "Cultural tourism includes movements of persons for essentially cultural motivations such as study tours, performing arts and other cultural tours, travel to festivals and other cultural events, visit to sites and monuments, travel to study nature, folklore or art or pilgrimages'.

It has been found that often there is an interplay of both cultural as well as heritage tourism features in destinations which is the case found at Hirapur.

Peoria et al (2001) defines Heritage tourism as "a phenomenon based on tourists motivations and perceptions rather than on specific site attributes…Heritage tourism is a subgroup of tourism, in which the main motivation for visiting a site is based on place's heritage characteristics according to the tourist's perception of their own heritage'. In Nuryanti's (1996) opinion Heritage tourism =...is characterized by two seemingly contradictory phenomena; the unique and the universal. Each heritage site has unique attributes; but heritage although its meaning and significance may be contested, re-interpreted and even recreated, is shared by all'. Ashworth and Goodall (1990) stated that "Heritage tourism is an ultra compounded of many different emotions, including nostalgia, romanticism, aesthetic pleasure and a sense of belonging in time and space'.

Hargrove (2002) says that visiting the historic and cultural sites is one of the most popular touristic activity today. Families, seniors, groups and even International visitors choose to frequent historic attractions when on vacations. As a result destinations are paying attention to one of the fastest growing niche market segment in the travel industry today-Heritage Tourism. Lanfant M. L. (1980)argues about cultural heritage tourism that ?we are dealing with tourism with an all embracing social phenomenon characterized by the introduction of new systems of relationships in all sectors of activity, bringing about structural changes at all levels of social life and increasingly affecting all regions of the world".

Heritage tourism, as a part of the broader category of "cultural tourism", is now a major pillar of the nascent tourism strategy of many countries. Cultural/heritage tourism strategies in various countries have in common that they are a major growth area, that they can be used to boost local culture, and that they can aid the seasonal and geographic spread of tourism(Richards, 1996). The

Chausath Yogini temple is an embodiment of the venerated all powerful Divine female figure, the "Yogini". According to Gadon, the Bhauma-Karas ruled during the period when the Yoginis came into prominence, a dynasty of six queens that ruled along the Odisha coast. Anna Dallapicola maintains that the yogini's symbolize,"the forces of fertility, vegetation, illness, death, yoga, magic", all forces of Shakti. The term "yogini" has several meanings, according to Miranda Shaw (1994). Quoting Monier-Williams, Shaw states that the term can mean a female practitioner of yoga, or ritual arts, a female being with magical powers, or a type of female deity.

The principles of Sthapatya Veda (the Indian tradition of architecture) state that the temple and the town should be a reflection of the cosmos. The temple architecture and the city plan are, therefore, related in their conception. (Subhash Kak) The Hindu temple also represents the Meru mountain, the navel of the earth. In the Shilpa Prakasha, a 9th-12th century Orissan temple architecture text, Ramachandra Kaulachara describes the Yogini Yantra for the layout of the goddess temple. Alice Boner writes (1966), "The Hirapur shrine represents the creative expanding forces, and therefore could not be logically represented by a square, which is an eminently static form. While the immanent supreme principle is represented by the number one, the first stir of creation initiates duality, which is the number two, and is the producer of three and four and all subsequent numbers up to the infinite. The dynamism is thus expressed by a circular structure of the temple. "

This definitely is a pointer that Hirapur possesses all the trappings to be an ideal heritage/cultural destination of the future. Not only is it a crowd puller due to its unique architectural design, but also the combined effect of having been a tantra pitha and now the seat of worship of Mahamaya Yogini.

Traditionally identified as a place for the practice of tantra along with its associated rites and tiruals, it was avoided by the public who regarded the Yoginis as ferocious. With equal rights for women and emancipation of women being the agenda for the Government, the modern woman is a decision maker. She decides her life as well as her travel decisions. The contemporary world recognizes the spirit of religious diversity.

It is about the complex ways in which the cult of the Goddess expresses the concept of the female energy (Sakti), as a Mother Goddess, goddess of fertility, war and as one who causes and cures diseases (malevolent and benevolent), undergoing significant transformations from a dominant status in matriarchal/tribal societies, to a subordinate status, through incorporation and assimilation into the formal religions of a patriarchal society with a caste and class-based structure, and yet retaining its symbolism and metaphor i. e. its revolutionary potential for feminism and the struggle for equality in women's status down to the present day. (Jordan,Donna:Shakti's Revolution). The potentiality of Kali-like goddesses as cultural symbols in furthering diverse political causes in modern India relating to ecology, terrorism, nuclear arms and even nationalism is emphasised. Overwhelming evidence for the emergence of a Sakta counter culture occurs only after the 12 century AD leading to the Tantric Vamachara and Kaulamarga cults of the Brahmanical and Sramanic Buddhist (Vajrayana) and Jain (Yogini cult) and the Hindu Sahajiya.

The undue importance given to the Islamic invasions (8 century to 17 centuries) for the emergence of the Tantric cults, ignores the changing trends within the religious history of this period, due to the incorporation of various economic, ethnic and tribal groups into the brahmanical order as lower castes. This also necessitated the revival of earlier fierce, autonomous, tribal goddesses of protection and destruction as the Yoginis, Yakshis and Dakinis of a counter tradition. The Yoginis were never "spousified" and the Yogini temples of medieval times occur only in the tribal belt of north east, Bengal, southern Uttar Pradesh, Orissa, Madhya Pradesh and Rajasthan, with a rare example in the Coimbatore district of Tamil Nadu.

Depite the religious liberalism, Yoginis are now popular among the modern women as liberated Goddesses who had their own stance in society despite prescribed social sanctions. In this perspective it's interesting to note the number of tours to Hirapur led by the transnationalist, feminist,spiritually oreinted Goddess movement. There are many women's only travel packages to Goddess sites which celebrate the sacred Feminine.

Women awakening to their feminine power is beneficial for all of humanity. As women discover their feminine aspects this has very positive effect on men, as it opens them to the concept of the Divine Feminine/ Christ Consciousness and allows them to become aware of nurturing and receptivity. Through this we are able to support each other to live and express our true potential. Sacred Mystical Journeys has designed a Women-Only Goddess Tour, led by a special female guide who works with the Sacred Feminine and Goddess Sites of Ireland.
(http://sacredmysticaljourneys. com/ten-reasons-go-womens-tour/).

The Chausath Yogini temple has immense potential to be a major tourist destination in Odisha., identified as a cultural/heritage site of importance. The "Tantra" tag, iconography and the unique structure of the temple are definite crowd-pullers and hence need to be preserved. Rare in its history as a place of religious and occult practices of medieval times, it is an architectural wonder as well.

- A hypaethral(roofless) temple, the smallest among all Yogini temples
- The sixty four yogini statues along with their significant hair-do, ornaments and Vahanas (Mounts)
- Place of worship of Mahamaya Yogini
- A symbol of amalgamation of Shaktism (worship of the Mother Goddess) and the Vajrayana, or Tantric form of Mahayana Buddhism

It could be promoted as a part of the Bhubaneswar-Puri circuit as it is strategically located on the outskirts of the capital city of Odisha. All three destinations offer a rare blend of culture and heritage. Staged events and special interest tourism events can be effectively used to further popularize the destination. Events like the Chausath Yogini Mahotsav highlight the cultural significance of the ancient Chausathi Yogini temple. The festival show-cases dance, music and literary presentations by performers from all over the world. In essence it is a cultural re-awakening of the yogini cult.

Sensitizing programs of school going students initiated by Indian National Trust for Art and Cultural Heritage:

INTACH organizes several activities at the site among school and college children to generate awareness, like open-air classroom in the site, quiz competitions, dance and music performances depicting the history and heritage of the temple.

Other innovative initiatives like the Temple Stay program can be implemented to enhance attractiveness and competitiveness of the site.

However, inadequate infrastructure development initiatives by the state government is a clear hurdle. The destination needs to prepare itself for tourists and so requires better connectivity, provision for basic amenities, accommodation, food and shopping facilities etc. The State Government's proposal for a Rural tourism project for developing the site as a heritage village has been stalled. If it is implemented, it would easily lead to the beautification of the destination as well as setting up of the proposed amenity centre and crafts centre.

Contemporary research highlights the recent popularity of the modern Goddess movement and prominence of the ferocious Goddesses in warding off evil. This is in keeping with the worldly-wise modern woman who is assertive, can fend for herself and can take her own decisions. The Goddess is the missing piece of life's puzzle of predicaments. Motivators for women travelers to visit Hirapur could be the following:

Experience local (traditional) Culture

Spend leisure time in temple premises, amidst heritage and cultural attributes

Interest in History, Archeology and the tantric, yogini cult

Escape from daily routine, for relieving tension and fatigue

To have an opportunity for self-reflection(identity tourism)

Appreciation of rural scenery
Interest in religion, philosophy

Few tour groups have brought groups of women travelers to Hirapur on "Goddess or Spiritual tours". These are innovatively designed tour packages which combine heritage, culture, religion and mysticism for the seekers of peace and identity. There is a sense of connecting with the sacred powers. The following tour options are already available. www. spiritualjourneys. net

http://sandpebblestours. com/chausathi-yogini-temple-a-place-of-wondrous-occult/. enders

A combination of all these factors renders this site as an ideal tourist destination for the future and envisions its continued presence. An extremely niche destination, this site would be frequented by persons seeking a renewed identity.

Chausathi Yogini Shrine at Hirapur

This temple is famed to have been built by the queen Hiradevi of Brahma dynasty during 9th century AD. The wave of tantrism was at its peak then and the Bhoumakaras were ruling during that period.

The entire structure of the temple is made of a type of sandstone which was probably available locally and images are carved from chlorite. The passage into the temple in the east measures 8' in length and 2'6" in breadth. In the middle of the circular enclosure there is an open square mandap, the upper portion of which shows has been reconstructed by archeological survey of India. The mandap has openings to all our sides. While the niches in the inner enclosure contain images of Yoginis, the mandap contains the images of Bhairavas. In the Yogini cult, Siva is known as Bhairav, a guardian protector who symbolizes the powers of the Vedic Gods, Agni or Fire and Rudra or Thunder & Lightening. There are ferocious images of Katyayani in the outer circle of the temple. Katyanis were war goddesses to help Durga in her fight against Mahisasura and his allies.

64 Yoginis at Hirapur

1. CHANDRIKA

A four armed figure standing in tribhanga pose on a corpse lying prostrate at the feet. Tribhanga, literally meaning breaking in three parts, consists of three bends in the body, at the neck, waist and knee;hence the body is oppositely curved at waist and neck which gives it a gentle "S" shape and is considered the most graceful and sensual of the Odissi dance positions.

Braided hair over her head, the statue is adorned with ornaments – anklets, girdle, necklace and ear ornaments adorn most Yoginis.

2. TARA

A two armed figure, mounted on a corpse in bent knee pose. The braid of hair to the left is popularly known as Keshabandha. The strands of hair are neatly combed and arranged into various conical forms of a series of diminishing tiers and placed in position by tying up the arrangement securely. Various ornaments for the head and other ornaments like armlets, anklets, girdle necklace and kappa are found.

3. NARMADA

Two armed, she stands on an elephant and wears a garland of skulls or mundamala as well as various ornaments. She holds a skull-cup like kapala near to her mouth and is believed to be drinking blood. Hair is braided to the right of her head.

4. YAMUNA

Four armed, the figure stands in the pratyalidha pose.

The mount is a big tortoise. Her curling hair is raised over the head known as Jatamandala. Long strands of thick hair woven into three braids are wound in circular forms and held behind on the neck like a disc or a fan. A skull-cup is seen in the upper right hand.

5. LAXMI/MANADA

Two armed, the figure is seen standing on a full blown lotus. The braid of hair is over her head. A noticeable piece of ornament is naga keyura (armlet of naga or cobra or serpent band). She is wearing a peacock feather skirt.

6. VARUNI

Two armed, the figure has hair braided to the left of her head. The pedestal symbolizes waves. Standing in a samabhanga pose, she is adorned with ornaments on the head and body.

7. GAURI

Four armed, Gauri stands astride an alligator. With a chignon on top of her head, she wears girdle, necklace, armlets, anklets and various ornaments on the head and is standing in a samabhanga pose.

8. AINDRI/ INDRANI

Two armed, mounted on an elephant, the figure has hair braided on top of the head and various ornaments decorating the head and body. She is standing on the pratyalidha pose.

9. VARAHI

Four armed with the face of boar, the figure is mounted on a buffalo. Armlets,, anklets girdle necklace and kappa with mukuta and kirita adorn the statue. She holds a skull cup and bow.

10. PADMABATI

Two armed and fierce, Padmabati stands on the hood and body of a serpent. Her braid of hair is over her head. Adorned with garland of skulls, she holds a khadga in her right hand.

11. ASHTAGRIBA/VANARMUKHI

The figure is four armed with a monkey face. There is a camel with a long,curled neck on the pedestal as the mount. She is standing in Dwibhanga pose.

12. VAISHANAVI

Two armed and with a graceful face the statue has curly hair and sarpa mukuta over her head, apart from the usual ornaments. Garuda as the mount indicates her to be Vaishnavi.

13. PANCHAVARAHI

This graceful figure is two-armed with beautiful braid of hair and a boar as the mount. She is standing in a Tribhanga pose with a benevolent smile on her face

14. VADYAROOPA

This two armed figure has hair braided over her head. She stands in a dwibhanga pose on a drum and has ornament on different parts of her body.

15. CHARCHIKA

Two armed statue has mount a male figure as the mount.

The male figure holds the stem of a lotus in his right hand. She is standing in a tribhanga pose.

16. BETALI

Four armed figure Betali has a fish as the mount and braided hair. A garland of skulls adds to her aura with ornaments like armlets, anklets girdle necklace and kappa. She is standing in a samabhanga pose.

17. CHINNAMASTAKA

This four armed figure has the mount as a severed head. Braid of hair floats over her bow in her lower left hand. She is standing in a dwibhanga pose.

18. BINDHYABASINI

This statue is two armed. The mount is like a flat roofed house or cave with a gap in the middle. Her face is a ferocious buffalo head with disheveled hair know as Jatamandala.

19. JALAKAMINI

This two armed figure mounts on a big frog. She has strikingly beautiful waist band and attire. She is standing in a tribhanga pose.

20. GHATABARA

A two armed figure, Ghatabara mounts a lion. She appears in a dance pose.

21. KAKARALI

A two armed graceful figure, this statue has a dog as

the vahana. Her right foot is held tightly by both hands and placed over her left thigh. It appears she is in the pose of adjusting her anklet.

22. SARASWATI

Standing upon a big serpent, she is a four armed figure. She has got moustache and appears to be twisting the same. A tumuru is slung on her shoulder.

23. BIRUPA

This two armed figure stands in a dwibhanga pose on a pedestal engraved with waves.

24. KAUVERI

This is a two armed figure with seven ratna kalasas or ratnanidhis on the pedestal. The Ratna kalasas are balanced over a full blown lotus on which she stands. Her hair is braided to the right with mukuta and kirita over her head. She wears a bejeweled girdle apart from other ornaments.

25. BHALLUKA

This statue depicts a two armed boar faced figure with raised hair in the Jatamandala style. A padmalata is engraved on the pedestal. She wears various ornaments and holds a damru in her right hand.

26. NARASIMHI

This four armed lion-faced figure has hair like the mane of a lion. She appears to be holding a pot on her hand. There are five flowers with leaves on the pedestal.

27. BIRAJA

A two armed graceful figure, Biraja has her braid of hair to the right, mounted on a lotus bud with leaves. She is standing in a dwibhanga pose.

28. VIKATANANA

This statue is a two armed ferocious figure with protruding lips and curling matted hair over her head. She is having sarpa mukuta type of hair style.

29. MOHALAXMI

A two-armed, graceful figure on a full blown lotus, Mahalaxmi wears a garland of snakes and holds vajra and a shield in both her hands.

30. KAUMARI

Kaumari is a two armed, graceful figure standing on a peacock. There is akshamala on her right arm and the usual ornaments like necklace, girdle and anklets. She stands in dwibhanga pose.

31. MAHAMAYA

A ten armed figure and slightly bigger then rest of the yoginis, Mahamaya is mounted on a full blown lotus. A squarish Shakti peetha is placed below her feet on the ground. She is adorned with a mukuta and kirita with a beautiful necklace, bejewelled girdle anklets and armlets. This Yogini is worshipped as the presiding deity of the shrine. The locals refer to the temple as Mahamaya temple and the ancient tank at the southern side of the temple is named as Mahamaya Pushkarini.

32. USHA/ RATI

A two armed figure with a ferocious expression on her face and raised curly hair in the Jatamandal style, this statue stands in a bent knee pose. In the pedestal there is the engraving of an archer with bow and arrow in hands and quiver on the shoulder.

33. KARKARI

The mount of this two-armed yogini is a crab. With the keshabandha hair style, ear ornaments, girdle and necklace, she appears in a tribhanga pose.

34. SARPASHYA

This four-armed Yogini has the face of a snake and is embellished with various ornaments. The pedestal is broken and so the vahana cannot be seen easily. She is standing in a dwibhanga pose.

35. YASHA/ JASA

A two armed figure with the mount as a cot with four legs, this Yogini is decorated with kirita and mukuta over her head known as jatamukuta. She is standing in a tribhanga pose.

36. AGHORA

This two armed figure has a furious expression with bulging eyes. The mount is a horned goat like animal. She is standing in a dwibhanga pose.

37. RUDRAKALI

Rudrakali appears as a two armed figure mounted on a cow. Her hair is spread all around her face like flame.

There is a sword in her right hand. With intricately designed clothes, she stands in a samabhanga pose.

38. VAINAYAKI/ GANESHANI

This is a two armed, elephant faced potbelly figure with an ass as the mount. She is wearing her hair in the jata juta (knot of matted hair) or jatamukuta style.

39. BINDHYABALINI

A two armed figure, standing on a rat with a beautiful braid of hair to the right of her head, Bindhyabalini holds a bow in left hand and bow string on the right and seems to be balancing the arrow. She is standing in a pratyalidha pose.

40. VEERA KUMARI

A four armed beautiful figure, mounted on a scorpion, this statue has ornaments decorating her body. Her upper hands are raised.

41. MAHESHWARI

Maheshwari is a four armed figure, mounted on a bull. With the keshabandha hair style, she is adorned with various ornaments and standing in a dwibhanga pose.

42. AMBIKA

This is a four armed figure with two wheels as the mount with a mongoose below. Her hands lean against both the knee joints as she is in a bent knee pose. She is holding a damru in her upper right hand.

43. KAMAYANI

This Yogini is a two-armed statue with a cock as her

pedestal. She is adorned with various ornaments and standing in a dwibhanga pose.

44. GHATABARI

This two armed figure is mounted on a lion in a dwibhanga pose. She has curling hair over her head with ornaments known as karanda mukuta.

45. STUTEE

This yogini statue is a four armed figure mounted on a haladi kathua. (Pot to keep turmeric paste). A flower vase is also engraved on the pedestal. Braid of hair is to the right with flower garlands adorned with various ornaments and mukuta. She is standing in the samabhanga pose.

46. KALI

This is a two armed figure mounted on a male body, holding a trident. The male figure is wearing mukuta and kirita and has a third eye, identified to be lord Shiva. She is standing in a dwibhanga pose.

47. UMA

Uma is a graceful, four armed figure with mukuta and kirita /jata mukuta over her head, holding a "naga phasha" in her upper left hand with the lower left arm is in abhaya mudra. Lotus flowers constitute her mount.

48. NARAYANI

A two armed graceful figure, Narayani has her left hand upon a madya bhanda (wine keg) and holds a sword in the right hand. With a kesha bandha hair style, she has various ornaments as her decorations. The pedestal is an earthen pot having a conical lid.

49. SAMUDRA

A two armed figure with the braid of hair to the left, a tiara on her head and various ornaments on her body Samudra has a conch shell with two legs as the mount. She is standing in a dwibhanga pose.

50. BRAHMANI

This four armed and three faced figure, with kirti and mukuta or jata and sacred thread and ornaments adorning her body, Brahmani has a book as the mount. At the left end of the pedestal a majestic lion is carved with beads in its mouth.

51. JWALAMUKHI

A two armed figure mounted on a platform with eight legs, her ears are raised and long. Two long knots of matted hair are found hanging on both sides of her head. She stands in a dwibhanga pose.

52. AGNIHOTRI

Two armed figure standing on a ram, this Yogini holds a sword in the raised right hand. She is adorned with various ornaments. The flames of fire surround her.

53. ADITI

Two armed with a chignon on top, Aditi has a parrot on the pedestal as the mount She stands in a samabhanga pose.

54. CHANDRAKANTI

Two armed figure mounted on wooden cot with four legs, this staute wears her hair in the Keshabandha style along with various ornaments. She stands in a dwibhanga pose.

55. VAYUBEGA

A two armed graceful figure, with a chignon over her head, Vayubega has a female yak as her mount.

56. CHAMUNDA

This four armed awe-inspiring figure, with a skeletal body and dangling breasts, Chamunda is wearing a garland of skulls. She holds a lion hide over her head. In the lower two hands she holds a katari and a severed human head. The musk deer is the mount of this ferocious yogini standing in the tribhanga pose.

57. MURATI

Murati is a two armed figure mounted on a horned deer and the braid of hair spread out like flames. Bejewelled with various ornaments she stands in tribhanga pose.

58. GANGA

A four armed figure standing upon the back of Makara, she is adorned with various ornaments. She holds the stalk of a full blown lotus in her upper right hand and a naga phasha in her lower left. She is standing in a tribhanga pose.

59. DHUMABATI

This two armed figure is mounted on a duck. She

holds a fan in both her hands and stands in a samabhanga pose.

60. GANDHARI

A two armed figure mounted on a horse, this statue has a kadamba tree in the background. She stands in a samabhanga pose.

61. SARVA MANGALA

This is the missing Yogini with an empty niche. The statue of sarva mangala was housed here.

62. AJITA

This four armed figure has hair style appearing like flames. There is a stag on the pedestal as the mount. She stands in a tribhanga pose.

63. SURYA PUTRI

She is a four armed figure and graceful in appearance. She is mounted on a galloping horse. With kirita on head and various ornaments adorning her body. She holds a bow and arrow with a quiver.

64. VAYU VEENA

This two armed has hair braided to the right of her head. Adorned with various ornaments and intricate earrings known as kappa, she appears resplendent on a pedestal with an engraving of a black buck and two flower vases.

The Hirapur Yoginis are extraordinarily beautiful figures with exquisitely carved features and sensuously formed bodies. They are standing figures with elaborate ornaments of various types. A gentle maiden adjusting an anklet, exudes femininity and sensuality with her softly curved stomach, wide hips and elegant posture. Her slim, flexible figure is admirably portrayed, while her eyes, eyebrows and lips have delicate lines. The ornaments are highly ornate- the bracelets, armlets, necklaces, anklets, earrings, garland and the headdress. The hairstyles are also either a one sided bun or a coronet of interlocking curls.

Photo source: *Suresh Balabantaray*

From Tantra to Cultural Tourism: the new age traveller's alternative

The Chausathi Yogini temple situated at Hirapur has long been venerated as a seat of Tantra worship. The Tantric cult of the yoginis evoked awe and fear in the mind of villagers in ancient times. The cult of sixty-four Yoginis was the exuberant expression of extreme form of tantricism in about 8th century AD when the occult and esoteric Sadhana reached the highest peak. Over time, the cult lost its sway and was forgotten along with the temple and its rare statues.

The new age traveller is in search of authentic experiences. Researchers have argued that New Age spirituality is best understood as a form of 'self-spirituality' and as an expression of the consumer capitalist tendency to commodify all things, in the process converting religion into a 'spiritual marketplace'. (Ivakhiv). Odisha is successfully promoting its temples as destinations for temple tourism. Attempts must be directed to promote the Chausathi Yogini temple as a tourism destination of importance.

World's leading category of international trade, tourism, is increasingly offering a range of cultural heritage products, from visiting monuments to discovering unique ways of life as supply for increasing cultural and heritage tourism demand. UNESCO defines culture tourism as "to create a discerning type of tourism that takes account of other people's cultures" (UNESCO, 2005). Indeed culture and heritage tourism has been gaining importance recently not only for its economic gains but due to more sustainable approaches. As rural and regional economies go through difficult times of change, it may seem to some local communities that heritage can help in terms of economical gains.

Cultural tourism can be defined as the subset of tourism concerned with a country or region's culture and its customs. Cultural tourism generally focuses on communities who have unique customs, unique form of art and different social practices, which basically distinguishes it from other types/forms of culture. Cultural tourism includes tourism in urban areas, particularly historic or large cities and their cultural facilities such as museums and theatres. It can also include tourism in rural areas showcasing the traditions of indigenous cultural communities (i. e. festivals, rituals), and their values and lifestyles. Preserving cultural heritage appears to be a key factor in economic policies supporting tourism development.

Cultural Heritage Tourism

There is no singular, specific definition of either cultural or heritage tourism. Some call it cultural tourism, some heritage tourism, some cultural & heritage tourism or in short, cultural heritage tourism (Cultural & Heritage Tourism Alliance, 2002). Culture is a set of distinctive spiritual, material, intellectual and emotional features of society or a social group. It encompasses, in addition to art and literature, lifestyles, ways of living together, values systems, traditions and beliefs (UNESCO, 2001). The National Trust's definition of cultural heritage tourism is "traveling to experience the places and activities that authentically represent the stories and people of the past and present. It includes historic, cultural and natural resources. "(Cultural Heritage Tourism,2005).

Cultural Heritage can be identified as the ways of living, developed by a community and passed on from generation to generation, which includes the customs, practices, places, objects, artistic expressions and values. Cultural Heritage can either be Intangible or Tangible Cultural Heritage (ICOMOS, 2002). The cultural heritage includes both tangible goods and the intangible goods, like symbols and values, as relevant elements that contribute to an expression of community and individual identity that is both territorially and historically contextualized. (Montella, 2009a, 2009b, 2012, Barile, Montella & saviano,2011).

Cultural Heritage can be distinguished as below:
- Built Environment (Buildings, Townscapes, Archaeological remains)
- Natural Environment (Rural landscapes, Coasts and shorelines, Agricultural heritage)
- Artifacts (Books & Documents, Objects, Pictures)

Promoting Cultural heritage as a Tourism product

The Natural and cultural heritage sites are considered to be the region's most important tourism attractions and can be featured as the most important tourism product for any place. Strategies should be formulated to protect and promote the cultural heritage and create awareness amongst the tourists who would like to gain knowledge and learn about the insights of the heritage sites. Nowadays niche tourist prefers travelling to destinations which have higher importance to Cultural Heritage tourism. It has become a 'specialty segment' of Travel and Tourism industry. This form of tourism has become a learning arena for tourists who can interact with the locals, learn how to make local handicrafts, educate by knowing about the history of the place, communicate with all age groups and enjoy their local meals. It can be promoted through different social networking sites which are operated; word of mouth can also be used for promoting cultural heritage sites. The state government should introduce fairs and festivals, which can also benefit the locals showcasing the beauty of the places naturally through the local residents. Light and sound show can also be organized in a more innovative manner which can involve the tourists for their better understanding. Plays can be organized by the locals for educating the visitors about their culture and the importance which has been followed since ages. Promoting Cultural heritage does not mean only protecting and preserving it, it should not be fixed or frozen; rather should be promoted in other aspects as well and the state tourism board and the government should extend their help in making the cultural heritage promoted as a tourism product.

Marketing of Chausathi Yogini temple of Hirapur as a tourism product

Destination positioning

Destination positioning presents a form of market communication, and used in tourism marketing it enables tourist destinations to enhance their attractiveness and competitiveness through the development of a unique distinctive position compared to their competitors (McCabe, 2009; World Trade Organization, 2006; Selby, 2004; Buhalis, 2000). It is necessary to position this rare, ancient temple in a way which will enable potential visitors to picture and visualize the temple and the village of Hirapur in their mind as a distinctive place.

Using interpretative strategy

Making sites and communities come alive is the focus of this strategy. It can include instruction on how to tell the story of the site or community, understanding interpretive methods and how to attract and engage visitors.

This interpretation utilizes facts and embeds them into stories, which should enable a better understanding of the selected themes, and on the simplest level this should provide more effective communication (Carter, 2001). Examples of some forms of interpretation which can be used for marketing the Chausathi yogini shrine of Hirapur are brochures, driving tours, walking tours, museums, exhibits, audio tours and tour guides. Fairs and Festivals can be organized keeping in mind the theme and the culture of the Chausathi yogini shrine.

Marketing the Community's Cultural Heritage

This site can be promoted by collaborating with the tourism industry and by attracting visitors to their community or region. The local community's message can be defined and strategies can be developed using public relations, social media, advertising, tourism industry sales and other marketing tools.

Making the Community Visitor Ready

To market the shrine of Chausathi yogini, it is essential to understand the importance of visitor-oriented customer service, how the needs of tourists differ from residents, operating visitor-friendly retail establishments and cultivating hospitable front-line tourism employees.

Tangible and Intangible aspects of the Chausathi yogini temple

Heritage tourism comprises of two aspects- primary which is the main attraction and secondary which enhances or support the secondary aspect. Not only restricting itself to the monumental remains of cultures, cultural heritage as a concept has now come to include new categories. Today, we find that heritage is not only manifested through tangible forms such as artifacts, buildings or landscapes but also through intangible forms. Intangible heritage includes voices, values, traditions, oral history. This can be seen through the cuisine, clothing, forms of shelter, traditional skills and technologies, religious ceremonies, performing arts, storytelling.

The Chausathi Yogini Shrine at Hirapur was built under the aegis of Bhauma and Somavamsi rulers of Odisha and is the smallest in the group. Constructed as a hypaethral structure, it is distinct in architecture from Odisha temple architecture as well as temple styles in the rest of India. The temple is a circular structure, 30 feet in diameter, which is built of coarse sandstone and has barely 8 feet high walls containing 64 niches to house the sculptures of Yoginis or Dakinis (2 feet in height). The projected niches on the exterior of the edifice are studded with icons of "nava katyayanis" made of sandstone. But the ninth century structure is a beautiful site where one can really understand the architectural qualities of the Odia temple builders of that era.

"The 64 Yoginis are found in dancing posture. Most of them holding wine cup, Khadga and Vajra etc. are presented in ferocious forms. The central deity, a three-headed dancing Siva is a unique piece of art work. The temple at Hirapur, though smaller in dimension is of high artistic order. Made of black chlorite, the figures are in standing pose. The exquisite workmanship of these Yogini figures indicates the high artistic excellence and exuberance of the period. " (Gitarani Praharaj & Chittaranjan Mallia, Art Heritage of Odisha)

Odisha has preserved some of the most important aspects of its own cultural heritage. It is for this reason that the State has so much to offer the curious traveller who seeks to unfold new mysteries. UNESCO defines intangible cultural heritage as the practices, representations, expressions, knowledge, skills – as well as the instruments, objects, artifacts and cultural spaces associated therewith – that communities, groups and, in some cases, individuals recognize as part of their cultural heritage. In 2003, UNESCO adopted the Convention for Safeguarding of the Intangible Cultural Heritage, to recognize intangible heritage as a critical part of the global efforts to promote understanding and respect for cultural diversity.

Intangible heritage is becoming a 'learning arena' for tourists, where they receive information though formal and informal communicative channels from the local residents that are non-traditional and memorable. It could be, for example, learning to dance, sing, make handicrafts, and cook traditional meals, and participating in different rites, rituals, festivals and the like.

The fact is that the value of intangible heritage is defined by the communities themselves - they are the ones who recognize how intangible heritage is manifested. This is, and needs to be, a bottom-up approach. Tourism can help with this approach, raise awareness of the uniqueness and importance of intangible heritage, and strengthen a sense of pride among locals, while generating income for community members. The locals of Hirapur can educate the visitors with the existing knowledge they have and can also help them in collecting information about the yogini temple. This kind of niche tourism can be promoted well for the development of the local residents and making their lives easier by giving importance to the heritage site which they have valued, maintained and worshipped from generations. It can be a win-win situation.

A visit to the Yogini temple at Hirapur marks only the beginning of the journey into Odisha's mysterious past. It also throws light on the role the worship of feminine cults played in promoting harmony through the synthesis of major religious traditions of medieval Odisha.

Every year, Chausathi Yogini Mahotsav is being organised between 23rd – 25th December with dance performances related to Shaktism.

Despite war, terrorism, natural calamities and other major hindrances to travel and tourism, the tourism industry continues to flourish in several niche sectors. Alternative tourism refers to travel that is personal and authentic and facilitates interaction with the local culture, people and communities. The global travel community has been particularly interested in the "developing world" for authentic yet uncommon experiences An increasing number of world-travellers are in the pursuit of spiritual transformation in "less developed" locales of the world.

There has been a noticeable interest for Tantra Tourism among new-age travellers. From seeking one's identity to redefining leisure, the Nirvana- driven tourist finds Tantra Tourism to be a wondrous pursuit. Tantra is an ancient Indian spiritual practice, grossly mis-represented as an offshoot of backpacker or religious tourism. From the search for magic, mystery of tantric yoga to countercultural seekers Tantric Tourism has become a global pursuit. The new breed of travellers are travellers by choice, educated and adhering to unconventional beliefs.

The Chausathi Yogini temple is an ideal choice for such trails and tours.

Conclusion

Heritage is a comprehensive concept that consists of many diverse values. A well preserved heritage enables communities to learn about their cultural history truly and chronologically. Heritage is not a renewable resource and therefore it should be conserved in a most efficient manner. Heritage sites of small regions should be identified and be given equal importance. This would lead to promotion of the region and benefit the locals economically as well. The Chausathi yogini temple of Hirapur is of utmost importance as it is one of only four temples which exist in India. The architecture here is different from other temples and should be preserved for future generations and the intangible aspect associated with the temples must be promoted by the locals in form of plays and stories to educate the visitor and the tourists. The government has started with the Yogini Festival in Hirapur where cultural programs are performed like Dance, Drama, songs on yoginis to promote these temples and also for tourists to know the cultural importance of these temples.

References

1. Abbasi, A. A., and S. K. Tiwari. "Zoomorphic Forms", Dimensions of Human Cultures in Central India: Professor S. K. Tiwari Felicitation Volume. New Delhi: Sarup& Sons, 2001. 203. Google Books. Sarup& Sons. Web. 5 Jan. 2015.
2. APEC (2001), Best Cases on Tourism and Cultural Festivals in APEC Member Economies, LINE PIA Communications, Seoul, Korea.
3. Ashworth,G. J. & Goodall, B (eds): Marketing Tourism Places, London:Routledge
4. Boner, Alice, Principles of Compositions in Hindu Sculpture: Cave Temple Period, New Delhi: Motillal Banarsidass 1990 (Leiden: Brill, 1962).
5. Hollinheads, K. (2004) "Tourism and new sense: worldmaking and the enunciative value of tourism", in C. M. Hall & H. Tucker(eds): Tourism and Postcolonialism: contested discourses, identities and representations, London: Routledge
6. Kim, C. W. (2007), "Analysis of the Temple Stay. Korean Buddhism Cultural Organization. "
7. Shaw, Miranda,(1994),"Passionate Enlightenment: women in Tantric Buddhism", Princeton University Press.
8. Nuryanti, W. (1996). Heritage and Postmodern tourism. Annals of Tourism Research, 23(2), 249-260.
9. Richards, G. (1995). Production and Consumption of European Cultural Tourism. Annals of Tourism Research, 22(2) 261-283
10. Silberberg, T. (1995). Cultural tourism and business opportunities for museums and heritage sites. Tourism Management, 16(5), 361-365.

11. Zeppel, H. & Hall, C. (1992). Arts and heritage tourism. In Weiler, B. & Hall, C. (eds). Special Interest Tourism. London: Belhaven, pp. 47-68
12. Dr Swami Shankardevananda Saraswati, "The Importance of Shakti", YOGA Magazine, May 1999 London, England
13. Gates, Janice. Yogini: The Power of Woman, 2006, Mandala Publishing, p. 3
14. Nuryanti, W. (1996). Heritage and Postmodern tourism. Annals of Tourism Research, 23(2), 249-260.
15. Swami Vivekananda public lecture, Vedanta Voice of Freedom, ISBN 0-916356-63-9, p. 43
16. Shaw, Miranda,(1994),"Passionate Enlightenment: women in Tantric Buddhism", Princeton University Press.
17. Richards, G. (1995). Production and Consumption of European Cultural Tourism. Annals of Tourism Research, 22(2) 261-283
18. Silberberg, T. (1995). Cultural tourism and business opportunities for museums and heritage sites. Tourism Management, 16(5), 361-365.
19. Tate, Karen. "The Asian Sub Continent. "Sacred Places of Goddess: 108 Destinations. San Francisco, CA, USA: Consortium of Collective Consciousness, 2006. 203. Google Books. CCC Publishing. Web. 5 Jan. 2015. <https://books.google. co. in/books?id=b7KbLLjzuRgC&pg=PA398&lpg=PA398&dq=GAdon+Probing+the+mysteries+of+Hirapur+Yogini&source=bl&ots=US2khZctpc&sig=KLatY4MY7Tila05x9W0Oa5sX0cs&hl=en&sa=X&ei=LmymVIWbJIOTuASe64DICQ&ved=0CBwQ6AEwAA#v=onep age&q=Yogini& f=false>.
20. Tiwari, S. K. "Yoginis and Matrikas. "Tribal Roots of Hinduism. New Delhi: Sarup & Sons, 2002. 129. Google Books. Sarup & Sons. Web. 4 Jan. 2015.
21. Zeppel, H. & Hall, C. (1992). Arts and heritage tourism. In Weiler, B. & Hall, C. (eds). Special Interest Tourism. London: Belhaven, pp. 47-68

www.ingramcontent.com/pod-product-compliance
Lightning Source LLC
Chambersburg PA
CBHW071218070526
44584CB00019B/3065